# WORLD CLASS CUISINE

ARNA VODENOS PRODUCTIONS
Rockville, Maryland

SCARBOROUGH HOUSE
Lanham, Maryland

# WORLD CLASS CUISINE

## Tales, Tastes and Techniques from Europe's Most Celebrated Chefs

*Written and Edited by*

Gail Greco

*Senior Contributing Editor*

Jason Vogel

*Contributing Editors/Recipe Testers:*

Summer Whitford
Mark Fessenden
Ann Harvey Yonkers

*Pantry Recipes on pages 157, 161, 164, 165, 167, 168 by*

Summer Whitford

*Original Illustrations by*

Ralph Semsker

*Published by*

Arna Vodenos Productions
Rockville, Maryland

*Bookstore Distribution by*

Scarborough House
Lanham, Maryland

Schieffelin & Somerset Co., New York, N.Y.
Cognac Hennessy, 40% Alc./Vol., (80°).

Published by
ARNA VODENOS PRODUCTIONS
131 Rollins Ave., Suite 3, Rockville, MD 20852

Bookstore Distribution by
Scarborough House Publishers
4720 Boston Way, Lanham, Maryland 20706

Book Design: Kathy Whyte

Cover Photo: Dean Alexander
*Cherry Soup, Warm Scallop Salad, and Alsatian Onion Tart.*

Cover Food Preparation and Styling:
Summer Whitford with Mark Fessenden
Editorial Assistant: Tracy Bernstein
Copy Editors: Tom Bagley and Andrea Goodman

Wine Selections and Wine Tips: Schieffelin & Somerset Co.
Importers of the wines in this book
New York, New York

**Library of Congress-in-Publication Data**
Greco, Gail.
     World Class Cuisine / written and edited by Gail Greco with
Jason Vogel ; with contributing editors/recipe testers: Summer
Whitford, Mark Fessenden, Ann Harvey Yonkers.
          p.  cm.
     ISBN 0-8128-8555-4 : $16.95
     1. Cookery, International.  I. Vogel, Jason.  1959-
II. Title.
TX725.A1g723    1994
641.59-dc20                                          93-31660
                                                          CIP

Printed in the United States of America
First Edition/First Printing

**GAIL GRECO** is a veteran newspaper and magazine writer and editor, and the author of seven cooking and decorating books, including *Great Cooking with Country Inn Chefs,* a Book-of-the-Month selection. An award-winning journalist, she is a member of the American Society of Journalists and Authors and the International Association of Culinary Professionals. She is currently writing another book and speaking around the country on behalf of the DuPont Corporation's No-Stick Cookware Systems.

**ARNA VODENOS** is the executive producer and co-producer of the television series, *World Class Cuisine.* An award-winning television writer and producer, she has been featured in many books and newspaper articles as an example of young women entrepreneurs. Arna has many television shows to her credit and also produces the television series, *The Low Cholesterol Gourmet.* She is the creator and president of Arna Vodenos Productions.

**JASON VOGEL** is the senior producer and co-creator of *World Class Cuisine* television series. His travel publications include the book, *Hot Spots: All-Inclusive Vacations, and articles for Skin Diver, Underwater Worlds, Caribbean Travel, and Life,* as well as *The Washington Times.* Jason is also the creator/producer of the television series, *Spa Getaways.*

*All recipes edited and tested for American kitchens.*
*The majority of recipes were adapted for yields of 4-6 servings.*

*To Philip Vodenos, who captured
the joie de vivre spirit of
World Class Cuisine with his advice:
"Always be happy and never worry."*

*. . . and to Charles Gingold, whose
unflagging support and creative input
gave the project life, spirit, and vigor.*

# CONTENTS

# INTRODUCTION

## Setting the Table with the Promise of Romance and Good Taste

*The discovery of a new dish means more for the happiness of mankind than the discovery of a star.*
*— Brillat-Savarin*

This observation by French food writer and gastronome Jean-Anthelme Brillat-Savarin (1755-1826) perhaps best explains why a cookbook such as this one is so sought after. The old cliché that sagely preaches: You can never get enough of a good thing, remains unchallenged when it comes to great cooking. We search with enthusiasm for a new way to prepare our foods — a new combination to explore in our journey to adventures in good eating. And we look to the masters for the answers to solving our gustatory yearnings.

The enjoyment and essence of cooking, serving, and then sitting down to a fine meal have become very important — in a sense an art form. Eating together is again becoming a way of life; for eating — so it has been rediscovered — is a celebration, whether it's an everyday event or a special occasion.

As our palates have become increasingly sophisticated, we savor every delicious bite of a well-prepared meal, a meal that also holds the expectation of romance and enchantment. Food is often the pivotal destination — the reason for going. At the other end awaits an unparalleled feast that awakens and excites the senses.

With World Class Cuisine, another dimension is added to your culinary frontier. You hold in your hands the compilation of recipes from some of the most celebrated food artists this planet has to offer. You have seen them on the companion television series. Now, direct from their kitchens to yours, here is a host of special preparations to help you turn your dining room — even during a busy work week — into a romantic escape — company over or not. Making time to serve up something special just once a week, is strong medicine for getting through busy schedules.

With this book — daydreams of traveling to Europe for that special meal at a classic restaurant or intimate bistro overlooking a festive canal, a bustling square or a vineyard at sunset — will always be with you. As you explore the stories of these revered cooks, you will come to know them not just as culinary aficionados, but as real people — new friends eager to share their knowledge; to help acquaint you with the basics or enhance your already well-honed kitchen skills.

You will, in essence, dine at their tables by using their recipes. The text takes you away from the braising and sautéing to the romantic and the passionate as you visit a chef who runs a country cooking school in the heart of wine country; stop by a 16th-century farm house, bakery, and inn, and hear the story of how an Austrian chef met her husband there and never left; and be surprised by a three-star cuisiniere who invites guests to dine right inside his kitchen and learn by watching him prepare the evening fare as the orders come in.

In addition, you will hear about many cooking styles and philosophies from a chef who compares his work to that of a clothing designer and another who has changed his Old World menu to lighter fare without compromising tradition and gourmet ambiance. Meet a chef who is as passionate about gardening as he is cooking — selecting the daily menu based on what's growing outside his kitchen door.

Recipes (most of them for four to six servings) are easy to follow and are readily available in American supermarkets and gourmet shops. They will beckon you to grab a whisk and get cooking. A bounteous onion tart offers a hint of festive fare from Alsace as does a steak from Basque; a hen cooked in rice-paper bundles from

Belgium; a cold cherry soup from the Loire Valley; a pasta with arugula from the Tuscan countryside; an unusual grape strüdel from Austria; and a sumptuous turbot with basil and tomatoes from Provence.

The recipes are accompanied by a choice of wine, expertly matched to enhance each dish and further excite the palate. Food origins and historical accounts accompany recipes as do cooking how-tos and whys, and please find some basic recipes in our pantry section to further assist you in the kitchen.

When the sun goes down, we at World Class Cuisine know that although the stars are twinkling above, you will be enjoying newly discovered ones of another kind, as Brillat-Savarin suggests. We raise our glass to you with global cordiality: cin cin, bon appétit, salud, smakelijk, guten appétit. ❖

— *Gail Greco*

Venice ❖

Imola ❖

Florence ❖

Tuscany

ITALY

OLIVE OIL

EXTRA VIRGIN OLIVE
OIL
PRODUCT OF ITALY
NET 16 FL OZ

# ITALY

Penne with Sausage and Arugula . . . 15

Crêpe Pinwheels with Spinach and Ricotta Cheese . . . 16

Red Pepper Purée . . . 17

Ravioli Stuffed with Spinach and White Truffles . . . 19-20

Salad of Roasted Red Pepper, Mozzarella and Sautéed Shrimp . . . 21

Ravioli Florentine with a Smoked Salmon and Whiskey-Dill Sauce . . . 23-24

Turbot with Tomatoes and Basil . . . 25

Warm Scallop Salad . . . 27

Amaretto Custard . . . 29

Sea Bass and Veal Carpaccio in a Walnut Oil Marinade with Vegetables and
Olive Oil-and-Lemon Dressing . . . 31

Beef Carpaccio with Celery and Toasted Pine Nuts . . . 32

# Tasting Tradition in Tuscany
## *Chef Giovanna Folonari-Ruffino*
### RUFFINO'S TUSCAN EXPERIENCE, TUSCANY

*It was the Tuscans who forged the first link with the regions of the south of Italy through the opening of restaurants where Lucca oil, navy beans, and Chianti could be enjoyed.*

Tuscany, famous for its veal and other fine meats, is also recognized as the orchard and vegetable garden of Italy. The region's lush, fertile earth and undulating vine-covered hillsides, form the dramatic landscape where Giovanna Folonari-Ruffino has spent most of her life learning about and teaching the preparation of fine Tuscan cuisine.

Chef Folonari-Ruffino descends from two illustrious wine-making families dating back many centuries. Always conscious of this proud legacy, she mirrors her origin and family traditions in all of her recipes. In her cooking school, she strives to preserve her rich history while looking to the future for innovative techniques. True to her ancestry, Giovanna infuses each recipe with wine and always includes foods that are indigenous to the region. "Because we are blessed with a bounty of fresh ingredients, Italian cooking is a true celebration of the senses and a feast for the soul."

The penne pasta with country sausage and fresh arugula is a perfect example of how Chef Ruffino enjoys adding bursts of color to all of her dishes. The visual appeal of this radiant emerald tinted vegetable, combined with the creamy sand color of the penne and the deep sienna in the sausage, provides as much stimulation to the eye as the complexity of flavors will to the palate. Chef Ruffino's approach to cooking reflects her personality – energetic, bright, and personable. What she brings to the table is more than a recipe. It is, as she describes it, a lifestyle. "We grew up with the kind of culture that elevated cooking to an art. This type of cuisine does not come from something you learn in school."

As the sun sets and Giovanna travels home to her villa in Greve, she traverses the Tuscan landscape that has not changed for centuries – the old houses and the stone steeples – and she knows that she is an integral part of the taste, the times, and the traditions of Tuscany. ❖

# Penne with Sausage and Arugula

*Arugula, sometimes called "rocket," provides this combination with color
and an added burst of flavor.*

2   tablespoons olive oil

3   fresh, country-style pork
    sausages, about ³/₄ pound,
    casings removed

1   bunch arugula (about 6
    ounces) washed and dried,
    trimmed, and coarsely
    chopped

2   medium plum tomatoes,
    peeled, seeded, and cut into
    ¹/₄-inch cubes

¹/₂   cup white wine

¹/₂ - 1   cup warm pasta water

1   tablespoon butter with
    about 1 tablespoon all-
    purpose flour

1¹/₂   pounds penne or other
    medium-size (such as
    rotini) tubular pasta

¹/₂   cup grated Parmesan
    cheese

Pour the oil into a medium sauté pan and sauté the sausage for 2 to 3 minutes or until partially cooked through. Add the arugula and sauté until wilted. Add the tomatoes, wine, and enough of the water to make a sauce. Stir to combine. Add the butter and flour, stirring to thicken the sauce.

Cook the pasta in salted, boiling water until al dente. Drain and transfer to a large warm flat serving bowl. Add the sauce and the Parmesan cheese and toss to combine. Serve immediately. Yield: 6 main-course servings. ❖

## Wine Suggestion

**Ruffino Riserva Ducale Chianti Classico Riserva.** Riserva Ducale (The Duke's Reserve Cellar) is full of ripe perfumed fruit that harmonizes beautifully with pasta and sausage.

# Crêpe Pinwheels with Spinach and Ricotta Cheese

*Serve this with a mixed vegetable salad and the Red Pepper Purée on the next page,
and you have a delightfully eye- as well as palate-pleasing meal.*

## Wine Suggestion

The strawberry-rose blush of **Clivo** entices the eye and invites the first sip. Clivo is at home when matched with grilled meats, seafood salads, cheeses, and vegetables, and certainly the crêpe pinwheels.

### Crêpes:

- 3  eggs
- 5  tablespoons all-purpose flour
- 1½  cups milk
- Salt
- Butter

### Spinach and ricotta filling:

- 2  pounds fresh spinach, stemmed, washed, cooked and squeezed dry, or 1 pound frozen spinach, defrosted, and squeezed dry
- 15  ounces Ricotta, preferably skim milk, drained in a sieve for at least 1 hour or overnight in the refrigerator
- 1  egg
- ½  cup grated Parmesan cheese
- 5  tablespoons butter, melted
- Salt and freshly ground black pepper
- Nutmeg

Make the crêpes by beating the eggs in a medium bowl. Sift in the flour and season to taste with salt and pepper. Stir in the milk. Allow the crêpe batter to rest at least 10 to 15 minutes or overnight in the refrigerator. This helps prevent the batter from sticking to the pan.

Use an 8x10-inch nonstick sauté pan, preferably with sloping sides, to cook the crêpes. Melt a little butter in the pan and pour in about ⅓ cup of the batter. Swirl it around to evenly and thinly coat the pan. Cook the crêpe until lightly browned on one side, about 1 minute. Turn and cook for about 15 seconds. Slide the crêpe out of the pan and continue cooking until all the batter is used up.

To make the Ricotta filling, mix the spinach, Ricotta, the egg, and 3 tablespoons of the Parmesan in a medium bowl. Season to taste with nutmeg, salt and pepper.

Preheat the oven to 350°. Spread crêpes with the Ricotta-spinach filling, about ½ cup per crêpe. Roll in the edges of each crêpe about ¼ inch and then roll each crêpe in a jelly-roll fashion.

Butter an 8 x10-inch baking dish, large enough to hold all the crêpes in one layer. Place crêpes into the dish. Cover with aluminum foil and bake for about 15 minutes or until the crêpes are firm but still moist. Allow to cool and firm up (about 15 minutes).

Raise the oven temperature to 450°. Slice each crêpe into 2-inch pieces. Arrange cut-side-up, in the same baking dish. Pour the melted butter over them and sprinkle with the remaining Parmesan.

Bake the crêpes for 5 to 7 minutes or until warmed through. The butter will be bubbling and the cheese melted. Serve with red pepper purée. Yield: 6 main-course servings. ❖

# Red Pepper Purée

*A delicious sauce for the Crêpe Pinwheels, the purée may also be used over your favorite pasta.*

2  *large red bell peppers*
¼  *cup olive oil*
1  *medium onion, thinly sliced*
2  *cups chicken stock*

Preheat the oven to 450°. Place the peppers on center rack and bake for about 10 to 15 minutes or until soft and blistered. Remove from the oven and put in a paper bag for about 10 minutes to steam. Peel the peppers under cold running water. Discard stem, seeds, and peel. Chop coarsely.

Heat the oil in a medium sauté pan or skillet. Add the onion and sauté over low heat until softened, about 5 to 6 minutes, stirring frequently. Add the red pepper and stock, and cook over medium heat for about 20 to 30 minutes or until almost all the liquid has evaporated.

Whirl the peppers in a food processor or a blender until smooth. Serve with the crêpe pinwheels. Yield: 2 cups. ❖

# Serving Food Fit for a King in Your Own Dining Room
## *Chef Valentino Marcattilii*
### RISTORANTE SAN DOMENICO, IMOLA

Having the opportunity to cook up dishes that were inspired by centuries-old recipes adds to the reward of entertaining guests. At San Domenico Restaurant, near Bologna in the Emilia-Romanga region of Italy, they know very well what a good feeling it is to serve dishes of the ages, for they do it every day.

Preparing, for example, the easy but unusual Ravioli Stuffed with Spinach and White Truffles followed by the splendid Salad of Roasted Red Pepper, Mozzarella, and Sautéed Shrimp will offer your own guests something special at your home.

Add an entrée and some interesting facts about the dishes, and you will open the door for conversation among your friends right on through a dessert of your choice.

As you set the large ravioli down in front of each guest, you may begin to whet their appetite by saying that this special pasta was a favorite of the final reigning monarch of Italy. Now, cooked up by San Domenico's Chef Valentino Marcattilii, it is no less regal. The recipe was passed along by Chef Nino Bergese, who tutored Valentino in the art of food fit for a king.

Since the restaurant opened in 1970, it has been serving noblemen and celebrities. "We try to reproduce the cuisine of the rich noble Italian families," explains Chef Marcattilii.

Once you have courted your guests with this lively information, you may want to grate some fresh cheese over their pasta. And why not let it be the best – Parmigiano-Reggiano, a cheese produced in the same region where Chef Marcattilii cooks. Then you can bid your guests, "Ciao," as you settle back in time to toast Valentino and San Domenico. ❖

# Ravioli Stuffed with Spinach and White Truffles

*Extremely flavorful, white truffles grow in Italy in areas such as Piedmont and Alba.*
*Trained dogs, sows, and even goats are used to sniff out the subterranean fungus.*

## Wine Suggestion

This dish pairs with **Ruffino Libaio.** Such an elegant recipe requires a wine of refinement and complexity. Libaio's richness comes from a blend of Chardonnay and Pinot Grigio grapes, which when combined with this dish will leave a feeling of balance and refreshment.

**Pasta:**

4  (6 x 12-inch) sheets of fresh egg pasta or 3¾ to 4 cups all-purpose flour

5  eggs

**Filling:**

8  ounces fresh spinach, washed, stemmed, cooked, and squeezed dry or ¼ cup frozen spinach, defrosted and squeezed dry

¼  cup Ricotta, preferably skim milk, drained in a sieve for at least 30 minutes or overnight in the refrigerator

¾  cup grated Parmesan cheese

5  eggs

⅛  teaspoon nutmeg

  Salt and freshly ground black pepper

4  ounces white truffles or ½ cup sliced wild mushrooms

4  ounces melted butter or truffle oil

(If you are using pre-made pasta, skip the steps for making fresh egg pasta.)

Make the pasta for the ravioli by mounding the flour on a work surface or in a bowl. Make a well in the center and break the eggs into the well. Beat the eggs with a fork, incorporating the flour slowly until it forms a dough. You may not need all the flour. Use just enough to permit you to gather the dough into a ball.

Knead the dough for about 4 minutes or until it is smooth and elastic, adding more flour as necessary to keep it from sticking. Wrap the dough in plastic wrap and allow it to rest for at least 30 minutes before working with it.

(You can also make the pasta in a food processor. Put 3 cups of the flour in the bowl of a food processor and add the eggs. Process 10 seconds to combine. With the motor running, add as much of the remaining flour as necessary to make a smooth dough. Wrap the dough in plastic wrap and allow it to rest for at least 30 minutes before working with it.)

Roll out the dough by starting with the pasta machine set at the widest setting. Cut the dough into quarters and shape into 4 disks. Choose 1 disk and cover the others while you are working to prevent them from drying out.

Feed the disk through the pasta machine rollers. Fold it in half and repeat the process. Do this about 10

*(continued)*

19

times to knead and smooth the dough. Narrow the setting 1 notch and feed the dough through the roller. Continue narrowing the rollers, notch by notch, until the sheet of dough is about 1/8-inch thick. Place it on a floured surface, cover, and continue with the other disks of dough until all the pasta is ready. Cover the dough with kitchen towels or plastic wrap until you are ready to use it.

To make the stuffing, put the spinach and Ricotta into a small bowl and stir to combine. Add the Parmesan, 1 egg, nutmeg, and salt and pepper to taste. Stir together until the mixture is smooth and thoroughly combined. Put the stuffing into a pastry bag fitted with a large tip.

Spread out 1 sheet of egg pasta. Pipe (2), 3 1/2 to 4-inch rings of filling onto the sheet of pasta. The rings should be about 1 inch high and spaced evenly so you can make (2), 4-inch ravioli from each sheet. Break an egg, pour off about half of the egg white and put it into the center of one of the spinach-Ricotta rings. Continue to fill each of the spinach-Ricotta rings with the remaining eggs.

Use a pastry brush to spread water on the pasta around each spinach-Ricotta ring. Cover with a second sheet of pasta and shape it around each large ravioli, pressing to seal. Put a 4-inch bowl upside down over the ravioli and use it as a guide for cutting with a pastry wheel or use a large, 4-inch cookie cutter to cut the ravioli. Repeat the process and make 2 more ravioli.

Bring a large low saucepan of salted water to a boil and cook the ravioli for about 1 1/2 minutes or until al dente. Use a slotted spoon to transfer the ravioli to individual warm deep soup plates. Shave fresh truffle over each ravioli using a vegetable peeler and sprinkle with the remaining Parmesan.

Pour the melted butter over the ravioli and serve immediately. Yield: 4 large ravioli for an appetizer. ❖

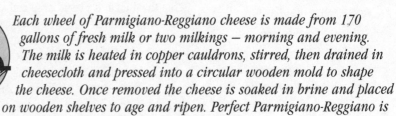

*Each wheel of Parmigiano-Reggiano cheese is made from 170 gallons of fresh milk or two milkings — morning and evening. The milk is heated in copper cauldrons, stirred, then drained in cheesecloth and pressed into a circular wooden mold to shape the cheese. Once removed the cheese is soaked in brine and placed on wooden shelves to age and ripen. Perfect Parmigiano-Reggiano is firm-textured and straw-colored with pale flecks.*

# Salad of Roasted Red Pepper, Mozzarella and Sautéed Shrimp

*Refreshing describes the blending of this gourmet light salad that can be served as an appetizer or as a luncheon plate.*

3  medium red bell peppers

³/₄ -1  pound fresh Mozzarella

¹/₂  bunch of arugula (about 4 ounces) trimmed, carefully washed, spun dry and torn into bite-size pieces

¹/₂  bunch frissée (or chicory) (about 4 ounces) washed, spun dry and torn into bite-size pieces

¹/₃  cup olive oil

1¹/₂  pounds medium shrimp, peeled and deveined

Salt and freshly ground pepper

Preheat the oven to 450°. Roast the peppers on a middle oven rack for about 10 to 15 minutes or until soft and blistered. Remove from the oven and put them in a plastic bag for about 10 minutes to steam. Peel the pepper under cold running water. Discard stem, seeds, and peel. Spread the pepper out on a work surface and, using a biscuit cutter, cut the pulp into 2-inch disks. You will need 3 disks of red pepper per salad.

Cut the Mozzarella into ¹/₄-inch slices and then cut 2-inch disks of each slice of cheese, using the same biscuit cutter. You will need 3 disks of Mozzarella per salad.

Arrange the pepper and the Mozzarella disks in alternating layers on a large salad plate. Pile a small handful each of arugula and frissée in the center of each plate.

Pour about 2 tablespoons of olive oil in a medium sauté pan. Add the shrimp and sauté for 2 to 3 minutes or until the shrimp are opaque but still tender. Season to taste with salt and pepper.

Divide the shrimp evenly among the salad plates and drizzle the remaining olive oil over each salad. Serve warm. Yield: 4 to 6 servings. ❖

# Wine Suggestion

**Ruffino Torgaio Sangiovese** is the wine that Florentines often drink with dinner at home or at an outdoor trattoria. A crisp and dry garnet-hued wine with a ripe berry flavor, it is versatile enough to accompany vegetables, cheese, fish, most spicy cuisines, and this recipe for the roasted red pepper salad.

# Cucina Verità and Storybook Days on the Grand Canal
## *Chef Celestino Giacomello*
### HOTEL GRITTI PALACE, VENICE

Processions of gondolas with their prows rippling the waters, 1700s decor, damask, silk, hand-carved friezes and ornate mouldings, all framed with a breathtaking view of the ancient Church of the Salute . . . This portrayal may depict something of a Renaissance fairytale, but it is the everyday backdrop for guests of the Hotel Gritti Palace. Add to it a menu of old-fashioned Venetian specialties and trend-setting cuisine, and the spell of Venice unfolds.

When visiting Gritti Palace, there is no denying the feeling of once-upon-a-time in a land far-far-away. But if you cannot hop the next motoscafo (motor taxi) to the palace, cooking up the chef's dishes is a way to bring the enchantment of Venice into your own home.

Chef Celestino Giacomello, whose innate culinary skills stem from a long line of family cooks, offers you two popular Gritti dishes. The traditional first-course pasta takes on a modern twist with its salmon filling and whiskey dill sauce, and the turbot is a marvelous main course.

"My style is to cook all fresh and well-garnished dishes, without too much sauce, butter, and cream," the chef observes, standing in what was once the home of Andrea Gritti, the 77th Doge of Venice during the 16th century.

A Risi e Bisi del Doge (rice-and-pea soup) owes its tradition to St. Mark's Day, April 25th each year, when the Doge had the first risi e bisi of the season. A pasta e fasiol (or fagioli) is also served here, consisting of tagliatelle pasta, white or red beans, and ham. The dish recalls when beans were brought to Venice by the Spanish conquistadors and became a mainstay ingredient of Italian soups.

The Gritti menu also has haute cuisine, and the chef's cucina verità or new, simple gastronomic interpretations, which might include shrimp scampi skewered and lightly fried in oil with a lemon and parsley sauce.

Gourmet ices – from sorbet to a Bomba Campiello – are still served at the Gritti in the tradition of 18th-century Venice. A watermelon sorbet is covered with chocolate and pistachio ice cream and lemon sorbet sandwiched in between. A chocolate gondola crowns the top. After biting into the bomba, you cannot help but live happily ever after. ❖

# Ravioli Florentine with a Smoked Salmon and Whiskey-Dill Sauce

*A fresh pasta dough stuffed with spinach and cheese is decidedly complemented with the unusual sauce combination of whiskey and dill.*

**Pasta:**
  2 (12 x 14-inch) sheets fresh egg pasta or 3¾ to 4 cups all-purpose flour
  5 eggs

**Filling:**
  1 cup Ricotta (preferably skim milk) drained in a sieve for at least 30 minutes
  4 ounces fresh spinach, washed, stemmed, cooked, squeezed dry and chopped, or one half of a 10-ounce package of frozen spinach, defrosted and squeezed dry
  2 eggs
  2 tablespoons grated Parmesan cheese
  Salt and freshly ground pepper

**Sauce:**
  4 tablespoons unsalted butter
  1 clove garlic, minced
  ⅓ pound smoked salmon, cut into ¼-inch cubes
  1 medium plum tomato, peeled, seeded, and chopped
  2 tablespoons Scotch whiskey
  2 tablespoons minced dill
  2 tablespoons grated Parmesan
  Olive oil, sprigs of dill, for garnish

If you are using premade pasta, skip the steps for making the fresh egg pasta.

Make the pasta for the ravioli by mounding the flour on a work surface or in a bowl. Make a well in the center and break the eggs into the well. Beat the eggs with a fork, incorporating the flour little by little until it forms a dough. You may not need all the flour. Use just enough to form the dough into a ball.

Knead the dough for about 10 minutes or until smooth and elastic, adding more flour as necessary to keep it from sticking. Wrap the dough in plastic wrap and allow it to rest on a counter for at least 30 minutes before working with it.

(You can also make the pasta in a food processor. Put 3 cups of the flour in the bowl of a food processor and add the eggs. Process 10 seconds to combine. With the motor running, add as much of the remaining flour as necessary to make a smooth dough. Wrap the dough in plastic wrap and allow it to rest for at least 30 minutes before working with it.)

Roll out the dough by starting with the pasta machine set at the widest setting. Cut the dough into quarters and shape into 4 disks. Choose 1 disk and cover the others while you are working to prevent them from drying out.

*(continued)*

## Wine Suggestion

**Ruffino Aziano Chianti Classico.** Medium-bodied and flavorful, this wine marries well with the complex character and variety of textures found in this ravioli dish.

23

Feed the disk through the pasta machine rollers. Fold it in half and repeat the process. Do this about 10 times to knead and smooth the dough. Narrow the setting 1 notch and feed the dough through the roller. Continue narrowing the rollers, notch by notch, until the sheet of dough is about $1/8$ inch thick. Place it on a floured surface, cover, and continue with the other disks of dough until all the pasta is ready. Cover the dough with kitchen towels or plastic wrap. Set aside.

Make the filling by putting the Ricotta in a medium bowl, adding the spinach, 1 egg and the Parmesan. Season to taste with salt and pepper.

Make the ravioli by beating the remaining egg and brushing the pasta dough with it. Put the filling into a pastry bag and pipe out rows of 1 teaspoon of filling every 2 inches of dough. Cover with a sheet of pasta and use a pastry wheel to cut 36 to 40 ravioli (2 inches square).

Melt 2 tablespoons of the butter in a medium sauté pan large enough to hold all the ravioli. Add the garlic, salmon, and tomato. Cook about 1 minute, stirring to combine. Reduce the heat and add the liquor, the dill and the remaining butter.

Meanwhile, bring a large pot of salted water to a boil. Add the ravioli and cook until al dente, about 2 minutes. Use a slotted spoon to transfer the ravioli to the sauté pan and add the remaining Parmesan. Heat the ravioli in the sauce, coating the ravioli. Arrange the ravioli on warm plates and spoon some of the pan sauce over them. Drizzle with olive oil and garnish with a sprig of dill. Serve immediately. Yield: 6 appetizer servings. ❖

# Turbot with Tomatoes and Basil

*Turbot is a flat fish which has been served at the tables of gentry for centuries.*
*Turbot, as with flounder, has many versatile methods of preparation.*

3 tablespoons olive oil

6 (4 - 6 ounce) turbot or flounder filets, preferably with skin

1/3 cup all-purpose flour

Salt and freshly ground black pepper

2 plum tomatoes, peeled, seeded, and chopped

1/2 cup chopped fresh basil or opal

1/4 cup sliced almonds

1/2 to 1 cup white wine

1/2 to 1 cup fish stock

1/2 cup heavy cream

Basil sprigs or opal for garnish

Tomato rose, for garnish, if desired

Heat the oil in 1 large or 2 medium sauté pans large enough to hold the filets in one layer. Dust the turbot with flour, shaking to remove the excess. Put the filets, skin-side-up, in the pan. Season to taste with salt and pepper. Sauté over medium heat for 1 to 2 minutes per side.

Add the tomatoes, basil, and almonds, and as much of the wine, fish stock and cream as you need to make about 3/4 of a cup of thickened pan sauce. If you are cooking the filets in 1 pan, you will need less liquid than if you are using 2 pans. Tilt the sauté pan back and forth, cooking over a medium high heat to evaporate and thicken the sauce.

Transfer the filets to a warm plate. Spoon some of the pan sauce over them. Garnish with a sprig of basil and a tomato rose. Serve with boiled potatoes dressed with parsley. Yield: 6 main course servings. ❖

## Wine Suggestion

**Ruffino Cabreo La Pietra** is a richly textured wine choice for the turbot. Made from the noble Chardonnay grape, it marries perfectly with fish in herb or cream sauces, or with veal and chicken.

# A Place Where Recipes Come from the Heart

## Chef Alfredo Del Peshio

### HARRY'S BAR, VENICE

Harry's Bar. The name does not sound like a moniker attached to a world-class restaurant, but make no mistake about this famous eatery in the land of seafood and gondolas. Harry's Bar is sought after by the locals as well as tourists for its continued fine cuisine, employing old family recipes first served to quench thirsts and satisfy the hungry with exceptional cooking.

Harry's still does that today as guests nuzzle up to small tables and stools, sipping such favorite treats as Bellinis, the bar's signature drink made with Italian sparkling wine and fresh peaches that are puréed by hand and mixed with the wine. The bar also serves Croque Monsieurs or Crunchy Misters. These are overstuffed sandwiches that ooze with seasonings, meats, and cheeses, and they are very popular.

But the likes of such famous individuals as Humphrey Bogart, Joan Crawford, and Arturo Toscanini, did not visit the bar just for its fabulous refreshments. They went also for its fuller meal service, the same reason celebrities still drop by for a bite to eat and the view of the Grand Canal.

And one of the dishes you might find on the menu is the warm scallop salad recipe you can now make at home. Chef Alfredo Del Peshio describes it this way: "Tossed with tasty flavors, this is a gentle dish that soothes the palate with its soft-as-clouds ingredients."

The Cipriani family owns the establishment and likes to say that their recipes are not derived from "a mathematical formula." Harry's Bar serves cuisine that is about "love — the love of food, of cooking, and of the people for whom you do the cooking." Is there a better way to describe the ways and the whys many of us enjoy cooking at home? ❖

# Warm Scallop Salad

*"Insalata di cape sante" is how they would say this dish in Italy.*
*Any way you say it, serving this combination warm, offers a light touch to this elegant dish.*

2   pounds bay or sea scallops
    Salt and freshly ground
    black pepper
5   tablespoons olive oil
3   medium plum tomatoes,
    peeled, seeded and chopped
    (about 1 cup)
⅓   cup flat-leaf parsley
¼   cup balsamic vinegar
2   cups sliced mushrooms,
    about ½ pound, preferably
    wild
¾   pound arugula, carefully
    washed, spun dry, trimmed,
    and coarsely chopped
    (about 4 cups)

Preheat the oven to 500°. If using large sea scallops, you may want to cut them in half or in thirds. Put the scallops in an 8 x 12-inch baking or gratin dish. Season to taste with salt and pepper and drizzle 2 tablespoons of olive oil over them. Bake the scallops for 6 to 8 minutes, stirring from time to time, or until they are opaque and somewhat firm to the touch.

Add the tomatoes, parsley, and vinegar to the scallops and stir to combine.

Heat the remaining oil in a medium sauté pan over medium high heat. Add the mushrooms and cook until golden, stirring frequently, about 6 to 8 minutes.

Arrange the arugula on 6 dinner-size plates. Spoon the scallops onto the arugula and arrange the mushrooms around the scallops. Spoon any pan juices over the salads and serve immediately. Yield: 6 main-course servings. ❖

## Wine Suggestion

**Ruffino Libaio Chardonnay-Pinot Grigio.** The blend of lush Chardonnay with the lively fruit of the Pinot Grigio works well with shellfish.

27

# Picture-Perfect Pâtisserie
## *Chef Gulio Corti*
### GULIO CORTI'S PASTRY KITCHEN, FLORENCE

If you have ever imagined opening a bakery to serve petit fours and sweet cakes, perhaps Chef Gulio Corti will inspire you. It was never his dream to satisfy the public's sweet tooth, but he is doing just that in his Dolci and Dolcezze or small pastry shop.

Here the eye is pleased as well as the palate with tortes, tarts, custards, chocolates, croissants, and a pie-safe full of wonderful confections. Chef Corti was a photographer before he opened his shop. But, in search of the most scrumptious, most delightful sweets to either eat or capture from behind the lens, he always wound up disappointed. "I couldn't get good pastry anywhere," he remembers.

To fulfill this passion, he started to sculpt and bake his own pastries. The sweets looked and tasted so good that friends urged him to open his own pâtisserie. He did, and today, runs one of Florence's most sought-after pastry shops.

The crowds flock to Corti's Dolci and Dolcezze because they can count on the chef taking no shortcuts when it comes to his passion. Being a photographer, he could not simply turn out a pudding or a roll without it being a picture-perfect creation. In fact, the chef admits he is a perfectionist, and says that if what he makes is not to his liking, "I throw it out and start all over again."

The photographer-turned-pâtissier brings to this already very artistic city, just another form of masterpiece that can be admired as well as savored – literally! ❖

# Amaretto Custard

*Dessert-making turns easy with this classic Mediterranean favorite.
The cookies are available in many supermarkets and gourmet shops.*

½ cup sugar

1½ cups milk

1½ cups heavy cream

2 ounces semisweet chocolate, chopped, or chocolate chips

2 tablespoons Amaretto liqueur

2 eggs

8 large double amaretti cookies

Preheat oven to 350°. Melt the sugar in a small heavy saucepan until it caramelizes. Do not stir until after the sugar begins to melt. Divide it among eight 6-ounce ramekins or eight 4-ounce Italian timbale molds.

Combine the milk, cream and chocolate in a saucepan and cook over low heat, stirring frequently, until the chocolate melts. Remove from the heat and add the Amaretto. When the mixture cools enough not to cook the eggs, whisk them in to make a custard base.

Place one half of an amaretti cookie in the bottom of each ramekin and pour the custard on top. (If using the smaller mold, you may want to use 10 molds to accommodate the extra custard.) Place the ramekins in a large roasting pan and fill the pan with enough boiling water to come halfway up the ramekins. Bake 30 to 40 minutes or until a knife inserted into the middle of 1 custard comes out clean. Allow the ramekins to cool, then refrigerate until ready to serve.

To serve, unmold the ramekins on a large dessert plate and surround with 4 amaretti cookies. Yield: 8 servings. ❖

*Caramelization is the chemical reaction that occurs when sugar is heated without water. It can be challenging to caramelize on humid days, because sugar attracts moisture.*

# Ricotta Fresh from the Shepherd:
# A Passionate Chef Fulfills Florence
## *Chef Annie Féolde*
### ENOTECA PINCHIORRI, FLORENCE

They wave to her as she putters by on her red motor-bike in search of the freshest finds for the daily menu. Chef Annie Féolde's early morning shopping at the market will determine what is for dinner at one of Florence's finest restaurants.

Enoteca Pinchiorri was founded by her husband, Giorgio Pinchiorri, who built the trattoria from a wine bar. Together the couple seems to have transformed the city's restaurant scene. By borrowing a little of the old with the new, Annie has added spunk and fabulous flavor to Florentine tables.

Chef Féolde offers three menus with one being the cucina creativa, developed from the daily market finds. It would not be unusual for her to return with fresh Ricotta from the shepherd who produced it. Another menu is based exclusively on fish – seafood out of the water no more than 24 hours; and lastly, la cucina toscana ritrovata, is gleaned from traditional Tuscan specialties Annie researched and adapted to make lighter and more acceptable to modern palates.

Amazingly, Chef Féolde has no formal training except working for her hotelier father in Nice. The chef began her career there, creating tasty delicacies to go with the wines her father served. A desire to brush up on her Italian brought Annie to Florence and she went to work at a restaurant to make ends meet. She met Giorgio, and it is said that this meeting not only changed the course for Annie Féolde, but also for Florentine dining.

Located in the Santa Croce area of central Florence, Enoteca Pinchiorri serves its splendid fare, surrounded by walls that date to the 15th century. A courtyard provides outdoor seating in warmer months. But whether outside or in, the setting is comfortably elegant and the service impeccable. Only those who saw her on the motorbike earlier in the day would remember that it took a chef's determination to personally track down the victuals to make her table d'hote so inviting. ❖

# Sea Bass and Veal Carpaccio in a Walnut Oil Marinade with Vegetables and Olive Oil-and-Lemon Dressing

*Carpaccio in a recipe indicates that the meat is served raw. Named in honor of a Renaissance painter, the concept is said to have originated at Harry's Bar (see page 26).*

### Seafood and meat preparation:

- ¹/₂ pound sea bass filets with skin
- ¹/₂ pound veal filet, well trimmed
- 1 medium zucchini (about ¹/₂ pound)
- 1 large carrot (about ¹/₂ pound)
- 1 bulb fennel (about ¹/₂ - ³/₄ pound)

### Walnut oil vinaigrette:

- 1 tablespoon balsamic vinegar
  Salt and freshly ground black pepper
- 2 tablespoons olive oil
- 2 tablespoons walnut oil
- ¹/₄ cup chopped walnuts

### Olive oil-and-lemon dressing:

- 1 tablespoon fresh lemon juice
- 4 tablespoons olive oil

No more than 1 hour before serving, slice the sea bass on an angle, as thinly as possible using a very sharp knife. If the slices are not paper thin, put each between plastic wrap and slide the blade of the knife over them, gently pressing and stretching the fish. Refrigerate the fish, keeping it covered, until ready to use.

Repeat this procedure with the veal. Do not pound the veal as it is much too tender. Refrigerate, keeping it covered, until ready to use.

Slice the zucchini in long, vertical strips or wide ribbons using a vegetable peeler. Repeat this procedure with the carrot. Cut the fennel across the bulb in strips, as thinly as possible.

Make the walnut oil dressing by putting the balsamic vinegar into a small bowl and adding salt and pepper to taste. Add the olive and walnut oils, beating with a fork to combine. Add the walnuts.

Put the sliced vegetables into a medium bowl and spoon 2 to 3 tablespoons of the walnut oil vinaigrette over them. Marinate 1 to 2 minutes.

Make the olive oil and lemon dressing by putting the lemon juice in a small bowl, seasoning to taste, and whisking in the olive oil.

Remove the sea bass and veal carpaccio from the refrigerator. Peel off the plastic wrap and arrange them decoratively on the plate, alternating the slices. Pile some vegetables in the center of each plate. Drizzle some olive oil-and-lemon dressing over each plate. Serve chilled. Yield: 4 appetizer servings. ❖

## Wine Suggestion

**Ruffino Orvieto Classico** is a versatile, almond-scented dry wine to complement chicken, veal, and fish preparations, such as the sea bass and veal carpaccio dish.

# Beef Carpaccio with Celery and Toasted Pine Nuts

*An olive purée, made with anchovy and olive paste, is part of this appetizer's tasty and unusual character.*

## Wine Suggestion

**Ruffino Chianti** complements the Beef Carpaccio with Celery and Toasted Pine Nuts. Michelangelo probably enjoyed some as he painted the Sistine Chapel! The Chianti region is surrounded by forests of pine, chestnut and oak trees, interspersed with vines and olive trees.

¼ cup pine nuts

¾ pound filet of beef, well trimmed

½ cup black, brine-cured olives, pitted, preferably Calamata or Niçoise

2 tablespoons black-olive paste

½ cup olive oil

1 flat anchovy

4 basil leaves, roughly chopped

1 tablespoon balsamic vinegar

Salt and freshly ground black pepper

3 celery stalks (about ¼ pound), cut thinly into 2-inch, matchstick-size slices

¼ pound mixed baby lettuces

Preheat oven to 350°. Put the pine nuts in a small baking dish and toast them for about 10 minutes or until they are golden brown. Allow to cool.

Not more than 1 hour before serving, slice the filet into 16 very thin slices. Put each slice between 2 sheets of plastic wrap and pound with the flat side of a cleaver or the bottom of a saucepan. The meat should be as thin as possible without tearing. Refrigerate the meat, keeping it covered, until ready to use.

Put the olives, olive paste, ¼ cup of the olive oil, the anchovy, and basil into a blender or food processor and purée until smooth. Season to taste with salt and pepper.

Make a vinaigrette with the remaining ¼ cup oil and the balsamic vinegar. Season to taste with salt and pepper.

In a small bowl, toss the celery with some vinaigrette. Put the lettuce in a medium bowl and toss with some of the vinaigrette, reserving some of the dressing for the individual final serving plates.

Arrange the lettuce on a dinner plate. Pile the celery matchsticks to one side. Remove the carpaccio from the refrigerator and peel off the plastic wrap. Arrange the beef on top of the lettuce. Add 1 or 2 tablespoons of olive purée to each plate. Spoon the remaining vinaigrette over the salads and garnish with pine nuts. Yield: 4 appetizer servings. ❖

Champillon ❖

❖ Epernay

❖ Paris

❖ Tours

❖ Joigny

# F R A N C E

Éguisheim

Rouffach

Monte Carlo
Côte D'Azur  Nice ❖❖
Antibes ❖

Country
Mustard

# FRANCE

# Cooking Up the Romance of a Lifetime
## *Chef Alain Finkbeiner*
### LA GRANGELIÈRE, ÉGUISHEIM

*"The measure of a good chef is not the quality of the ingredients he uses, but in his ability to work well with basic ingredients and produce a refined product . . ."*

*— Finkbeiner*

Once upon a time, the chef de cuisine had a sweet meeting in the kitchen that led to more than a croquembouche and a raspberry strudel. For Chef Alain Finkbeiner and his boss' daughter, a blending of hearts, tossed with a cup of desire and based on a sturdy crust of commitment, created a marriage and led to their very own restaurant.

The story has fairytale proportions. And that is how the lifestyle of the chef and his wife, Karine, and their La Grangelière Restaurant seemed to unfold. Alain was chef de cuisine at the Chateau d'Isenbourg in Rouffach when he met his wife. Together, they work at their restaurant – another story.

La Grangelière is housed in a beautiful, half-timbered house in the Alsace region that Alain and Karine rehabilitated. Its Tudor-style facade is punctuated by many window boxes that spill over with color and texture and have become the restaurant's outward signature.

"We were attracted by the charm of the village," remembers Chef Finkbeiner, of his first encounter with the old building. The chef immediately envisioned flowers, draping from the windows and began to dream. "I somehow sensed that this was going to be our restaurant."

Inside, convivial country tables set the mood in the brassiere downstairs. Upstairs is a gourmet restaurant. Both areas offer a blending of classic French with a touch of German. Éguisheim in the Alsace region is a papal town only a few yards from the southern rampart.

As chef and owner of the restaurant, Alain has realized his ambitions and strives every day to serve patrons, not only his fine cuisine, but with an atmosphere that offers them an experience. His dishes contain select ingredients, prepared simply and elegantly as his culinary philosophy espouses:

"The measure of a good chef is not the quality of ingredients he uses, but in his ability to work well with basic ingredients and produce a refined product. Indeed, you can use products such as cod and leeks, so ever present in a poor man's pot, to make interesting dishes. This is the measure of a good chef."

And measure for measure, the hard work and sharing of Alain and Karine makes this a magical place. ❖

# Alsatian Onion Tart

*A traditional cream-based appetizer with sautéed onions from Alsace,
this dish is great even for lunch, served with a fresh green salad.*

**Pastry shell:**

2 ½ cups all-purpose flour,
   chilled

1 teaspoon salt

½ cup chilled butter, cut into
   pieces

½ cup chilled margarine, cut
   into pieces

½ cup ice water

**Egg wash:**

1 egg lightly beaten with 1
   tablespoon heavy cream

**Onion filling:**

2 tablespoons vegetable oil

5 yellow onions, cut in half
   and then into thin slices

   Salt and freshly ground
   pepper

4 eggs

1 cup milk

5 cups heavy cream

⅛ teaspoon nutmeg

In a bowl of electric mixer with the paddle attachment, mix the flour, salt, butter, and margarine on low speed just until the mixture resembles coarse meal. Add the ice water, very slowly, with the machine on. Mix just until the dough comes together. (The dough should not be mixed too long or it will become tough. Make sure the dough is not too sticky at this point. If it is too wet, remove the dough from the machine, place on a lightly floured surface, and lightly knead in a small amount of flour to eliminate the stickiness. Never use too much flour with pie or tart dough or it can cause toughness and dryness. Also, any excess flour on the surface will burn in the oven.)

Place the dough in the center of a large piece of plastic. Wrap well and refrigerate for about 3 hours. This allows the dough to rest and chill, which makes it easier to roll out. After the dough has chilled, lightly dust the surface with flour and roll it out to a circle about 16 inches in diameter. Wrap the dough around the rolling pin and carefully roll onto a 10-inch tart pan or quiche dish. Gently pick up the sides of the dough circle and place them flush with the bottom of the pan. (The sides will hang over.) Take the rolling pin and carefully roll it over the top of the pan, shaping and trimming the scalloped edges clean of excess dough. Prick the bottom with a fork to ensure even baking.

Brush the egg wash along the inside of the tart shell and onto the top of the scalloped edges. Place in the refrigerator and chill for about 1 hour. Just before

*(continued)*

## Wine Suggestion

**Sichel Zeller Schwarze Katz.** Made from Riesling and Muller-Thurgau grapes, the *"black cat"* from the village of Zell possesses a flowery bouquet and a fresh fruit crispness that make it a fine partner to this mouth-filling onion tart.

chilled, preheat the oven to 350°. When chilled through, remove from the refrigerator and partially bake until the crust in the bottom turns pale golden, about 15 minutes or until the dough in the center of the crust is no longer raw.

When finished, set aside and prepare the onion filling. Heat a large sauté pan with 2 tablespoons of oil. Sauté the onions until just tender and season with salt and pepper. Continue stirring the onions to prevent sticking and burning.

In a medium bowl, lightly beat the eggs with a whisk. Add the milk and cream and whisk until well combined. Add the nutmeg and some salt and pepper to taste. Continue stirring the onions to prevent burning and sticking.

Remove the onions from the heat, stir to cool slightly and place in the bottom of the tart shell. Pour the egg mixture over the onions. Bake the tart 20 to 25 minutes or until the custard is set and the crust is golden brown. Yield: 6 servings. ❖

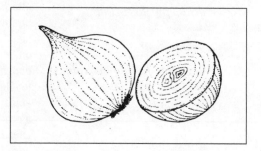

*Alsace is known for its many luscious fruits, including the renowned mirabelle, a golden plum that is indigenous to the region.* ❖

# Ravioli with Truffles and Bacon

*Freshly made ravioli, filled with this interesting combination of mushrooms and bacon simmered in a wine sauce, provides an elegant, easy meal.*

## Filling:

4  leeks, white part only

4  tablespoons butter

4  thin slices bacon, par boiled for 2 minutes and drained

2  small (canned) truffles, juice reserved

¼  cup port

½  cup heavy cream

  Pasta for 12 (3-inch) circles for the ravioli

## Egg wash:

1  egg yolk

1  tablespoon water

## Sauce:

1  cup chicken broth

2  tablespoons chopped chives

Cut the leeks julienne-style into 3-inch sections, then in half lengthwise, discarding the tender core, and cutting the remaining leek in long thin strips.

Heat 3 tablespoons of the butter in a saucepan. Dice the bacon. Cut one truffle julienne-style by cutting it into thin slices and then into strips.

Add the leek, bacon, and truffle to the hot butter and stir well to combine. Add the port and bring it to a simmer. Add the cream and stir to combine. Reduce the mixture over medium heat for about 10 minutes or until all the liquid has evaporated and the leeks turn to an amber color. Make sure they do not burn. Meanwhile, bring a medium pot of salted water to a boil.

Whisk together the egg yolk and 1 tablespoon of water. Brush the egg wash on one side of a ravioli skin, covering the entire surface. Place about 2 heaping teaspoons of the leek mixture in the center of each ravioli skin. Repeat the process until you have prepared all the ravioli skin. Fold each ravioli over in half like a turnover and pinch around the edges to seal in the filling. Use a 3-inch, scallop-shaped cookie cutter to cut through the ravioli skins forming a decorative edge.

Boil the ravioli for about 6 minutes. Lift them from the water using a slotted spoon. Drain them on a folded kitchen towel and arrange three ravioli per large dinner plate.

*(continued)*

# Wine Suggestion

**Sichel Bereich Johannisberg Riesling.** This wine is made 100% from the classic Riesling grape, one of the world's finest white wine varietals. Grown in the Johannisberg district of Germany, Riesling displays the elegant balance between ripe fruit flavors and crispness that is needed for such a fine dish.

Bring the chicken broth to a boil in a medium saucepan and whisk in the remaining butter. Add the reserved truffle juice and swirl to blend. Add the chives. Cut the remaining truffle into thin slices and place a slice on each ravioli. Spoon about ¼ cup of the chicken broth over each plate and serve warm. Yield: 4 servings. ❖

*Editor's Note:* *If you cannot find truffles, substitute with 2 large butter mushrooms.*

 *Truffles are a renowned French delicacy ripe with flavor. They grow in chalky soil or clay near the surface, and are very expensive since their production has declined due to deforestation.*

# Poetry and Philosophy from the Loire Valley
## *Chef Jean Bardet*
### JEAN BARDET RELAIS & CHÂTEAUX, TOURS

If Chef Jean Bardet could make a wish for all mankind, he might hope that everyone could enjoy eating at home as they do at his restaurant. That doesn't mean eating in a similar, Napoleonic house of white-sentinel columns with seating for 80, overnight rooms for weary guests, and acres of English country gardens, as at the inn. This great chef, who is also a philosopher of culinary pleasures, urges the savoring of food in any setting, by serving a communion of freshly prepared local dishes, complementary wine, and a cordial of an aromatic cigar.

Chef Bardet is almost apostolic in his approach to dining. Every aspect is methodic and there is great personal attention. The cigar at the end of the meal is a true gift from the chef. He finds that the tobacco assimilates the sugar in the dessert and complements the minerals in the wine to complete the meal with uncompromising satisfaction.

Eating is to the chef and his wife, Sophie, a spiritual passage of sorts. "We strive to bring a refreshing and life-changing experience to our guests — to offer them a new culinary dimension." That is how they define their mission.

Such a vocation requires an orchestration of the best there is to set their table d'hote with bounty from the Touraine region known as the "garden of France." It is no wonder that this self-taught culinary aficionado, who has earned two Michelin stars, also had a calling to be a priest and a musician. But wearing the toque instead of the collar allows Chef Bardet to do a little of each.

The chef's food bin is refreshing. "In France we have forgotten that the most beautiful recipes come from poverty, not luxury." Thus, he serves earthly ingredients, many of them coming from the garden of 500 herbs and vegetables he helps cultivate.

"A gardener lives with optimism," says Jean. "To be able to plant, to watch your product bloom, and to be able to eat it . . . it's an incredible experience." And it is added reason for also producing his own wines. "It's true that I love wine and each one has special characteristics. Each wine is like a friend to me. My biggest concern is to give them a role to play . . . to complement them with dishes that best suit them," he pontificates.

It seems fitting that this sage of many things culinary would select a dessert here made of choice red berries, pressed into a fruit soup that gently tickles the palate and expands the imagination. When served, it is likely to make your own guests, "each a friend to you." ❖

> *"In France we have forgotten that the most beautiful recipes come from poverty, not luxury."*
>
> *– Bardet*

# Cherry Soup

*This is the dish to serve company, either after the meal as a refreshing dessert,*
*or before the meal as a sweet introduction to a light meal.*
*You may use canned and drained cherries, but adjust the seasonings accordingly.*

*"A gardener lives*

*with optimism."*

*—Bardet*

2 ½  *pounds cherries,*
*preferably Bigareaux*
*or Burlat (Bing*
*will also do), washed*
*and pitted*
1  *cup water*
½  *cup sugar*
1  *scant cup freshly*
*squeezed orange juice*
¼  *cup freshly squeezed*
*lemon juice*
¼  *cup honey*
*Fresh mint for garnish*

Place the cherries into a heavy saucepan with the water and sugar. Cover and cook over medium heat. While the cherries are cooking, combine in a medium bowl, the orange and lemon juices and whisk in the honey.

When the cherries start to boil, remove the pan from the heat. Reserve the cooking juices from the cherries and set aside. Using a slotted spoon, transfer the cherries to the bowl with the juice and honey and stir well to combine. Reserve about ¾ cup of cherries for garnish. Put the cherry-citrus mixture into a blender or food processor and process in pulses adding a little of the cooking juices to help the blending. Process to a coarse purée and add more juice if necessary. The soup should have the consistency of thick syrup.

Remove from the blender or processor and put into a bowl. Refrigerate for several hours or until well chilled. The soup should be a nice deep pink. To serve, place 1 tablespoon of the cherry halves into the center of a 6-ounce bowl and pour the soup on top. Garnish with mint and cherries. Yield: 6 servings. ❖

*Vines have been cultivated in the Loire region since Roman times. The valley is divided into nine main wine-producing areas which grow a variety of grapes from Pinot Noir and Sauvignon to Muscadet and Gras Plant.*

# History and Tradition from the French Riviera
## *Chef Dominique Le Stanc*
### CHANTECLER RESTAURANT AT HOTEL NEGRESCO, NICE

The reception hall is decorated in Louis XIV style with gilded mouldings and chandeliers of brilliant Bohemian crystal. At the Hotel Negresco in Nice, amidst antiques and rare artwork, the culinary artistry of Chef Dominique Le Stanc is applauded with the same sense of tradition and history.

Having studied under renowned chefs since he was fourteen years old, Chef Le Stanc brings to the palate (at the hotel's Chantecler Restaurant), a regal mixture of sauces and seasonings, crowned with attention to detail.

As one of Europe's best young chefs, and a recipient of two stars from the Michelin Guide, he offers the gastronomic world a blend of tradition and new combinations. "My style is based upon experimentation," says Dominique. "I love to present my meals in a variety of ways." Note in the ravioli dish how the chef successfully married the artichokes and asparagus with langoustines for a romantic rendition.

The chef's skill in the kitchen has been likened to that of a composer at his classical instrument – fine-tuned, soothing, entertaining, but with a touch of bravado. This addition of pep and gusto defines him more like a Vivaldi, rather than a Beethoven or Wagner. Indeed, the blending of music, art, and fine cuisine, make up Dominique Le Stanc's exciting culinary repertoire. ❖

# Chicken Breasts with Fennel and Sundried Tomatoes

*A popular Mediterranean vegetable, fennel adds a light anise flavor to any dish.
Fennel can also be enjoyed raw or in salads.*

## Wine Suggestion

**Simi Altaire.** Pinot Noir, Cabernet Franc, and Pinot Meunier grapes conspire to create a wine with the seductive quality that the French call "gouleyant" (smooth and easy to drink) and offer a refreshing taste to help delineate the distinct flavors of this dish.

1   large fennel bulb, approximately 1 pound

4   medium artichokes

2   tablespoons plus ¼ cup extra virgin olive oil

7   sundried tomatoes

4   chicken breasts

    Salt and freshly ground pepper

3   branches fresh rosemary, with extra for garnish

1   small bunch parsley

Trim the stems from the fennel bulb and cut lengthwise. Then slice each bulb horizontally, to form julienne slices. Thinly slice the artichoke hearts into vertical strips, similar in shape and size to the fennel.

Pour approximately 1 tablespoon of the olive oil into a heated 2 quart heat-proof casserole. Add the fennel to cook (these take longer to cook than the artichoke hearts) over medium-high heat. Cook for approximately 5 minutes. Add the artichoke hearts and the other tablespoon of olive oil. Season with salt and pepper. Lower the heat and sauté the hearts and fennel over low heat for about 1 minute. Do not brown the vegetables; they must remain tender and moist.

While the vegetables are cooking, thinly slice the sundried tomatoes vertically to match the size and shape of the other vegetables. Season the chicken breasts with salt and pepper and insert a small sprig of rosemary into each breast by making a horizontal slice into the side of each breast. This adds flavor to the meat without adding extra calories or fat.

Add the sundried tomatoes to the casserole along with a branch of rosemary. Add more olive oil, if necessary. Place the chicken breasts in the casserole skin-side down. Cover the pot and continue to cook on low heat for an additional 20 minutes or until the chicken is cooked through and the juices of the chicken run clear. Turn the chicken breasts over once during cooking, making sure not to allow the chicken or vegetables to become dry or brown.

When the chicken is finished cooking, remove the casserole from the stove, take out the chicken and set on a plate. Add the parsley to the casserole and stir, replacing the lid to keep the ingredients warm.

Discard the rosemary from inside each chicken breast. Slice each breast diagonally into 5 slices. Spoon some vegetables onto each plate and arrange the chicken slices on top. Add a thin stream of the 1/4 cup olive oil between each slice and garnish with the remaining rosemary. Yield: 4 servings. ❖

*Editor's Note: If fennel is not available, sauté the sundried tomatoes and artichoke hearts with a small amount of Pernod to provide a similar flavor.*

*Cleaning artichokes can be easy, just follow these instructions. First bend back and cut off the tough outer leaves of the artichokes and slice off the top. Peel the stem and cut around the base. Remove any of the thick outer leaves that still remain. Cut the artichoke in half vertically and remove the choke; the furry interior that is inedible. This choke can be removed by carefully scraping the fur with a paring knife. Next, place the hearts cut-side down on a cutting board and slice vertically to resemble the fennel slices.*

*The edible part of an artichoke is the base of the leaves and the center, fleshy part or heart (once the choke or fibrous center has been removed). The variety of the artichoke most widely available in the United States is the globe artichoke. This is larger and tougher than the violet artichoke of Provence or the green artichoke of Florence, typically grown around the Mediterranean.*

*Meat should always be allowed to rest 5 to 10 minutes before cutting. This reduces the toughness of the meat and prevents the flavorful juices from being wasted.*

# Open Ravioli with Artichokes, Asparagus and Langoustines

*In this dish, the ravioli form the base for a capping of vegetables and seafood.*

## Wine Suggestion

**Domaine Chandon Réserve.** This rich, creamy, and complex sparkling wine is made according to the traditional méthode champenoise and is aged in the Napa Valley cellars of Chandon for a period of at least 4 years. Delicious with pasta, vegetables, fish, shellfish.

### Pasta for the ravioli:

1¼ -1½   *cups all-purpose flour plus additional for dusting*

2   *eggs*

2   *teaspoons olive oil*

8   *flat-leaf parsley leaves*

### Assembly:

1   *cup olive oil*

1   *bay leaf*

4   *sprigs fresh thyme*

8   *medium asparagus, woody ends snapped and lower stems peeled*

   *Salt and freshly ground pepper*

8   *langoustines or 12 large shrimp, or 1 precooked lobster, cut up*

2   *medium or 4 baby artichokes*

1   *lemon, cut in half*

   *Freshly ground pepper*

10-12   *flat-leaf parsley leaves*

   *Flat leaf parsley, as garnish*

Add 1¼ cups of the flour in a medium bowl and break two eggs into it. Add the 2 teaspoons olive oil and mix the dough with your fingertips, turning the bowl to help gather the dough up into a ball. If the dough is too wet, add as much of the remaining flour as necessary to enable you to gather the dough into a ball.

Flour the work surface lightly and knead the dough until it is smooth and elastic, about 6 to 8 minutes. Cover the dough and refrigerate it for about 10 minutes to allow the dough to relax so it will be easier to work.

Cut the dough in 8 pieces, flatten the first piece into a disk, sprinkle the work surface with flour and roll out the disk into an oval shape. Put a parsley leaf on the dough, fold it in half and continue to roll and flatten it. After you roll out the dough in one direction, turn it and roll it in the other way. This creates an even and thin dough and spreads out the parsley leaf making a pretty pattern. Trim each oval into a rectangle (3 x 5-inches). Continue to roll out the ravioli rectangles until you have made 8 and used all the dough.

Make an herb-flavored olive oil by adding a fresh bay leaf and several sprigs of thyme to ½ cup of the olive oil. (This olive oil is better when it is made the night before you are planning to use it as this gives the herbs more time to infuse the olive oil with their flavor.)

*(continued)*

Cook the asparagus in boiling salted water until tender but not soft, about 8 minutes. (Reserve the cooking water for later.) While the asparagus cook, remove the tails of the langoustines. Remove the meat from the shell and set it aside.

Trim the artichokes, removing them from the stalk and bending back and cutting off the tough outer leaves. Continue peeling off the tough outer leaves until you reach the light green center core of the artichoke. Cut off the top of the artichoke, peel the stem and trim the base to remove the tough outer fiber. Rub the artichoke all over with a cut lemon to prevent it from discoloring. Cut the artichoke in half vertically, remove the inner choke by cutting it out with the point of a paring knife, place it, cut-side-down, on the cutting board and slice it across into thin slivers.

Pour about 2 tablespoons of the unflavored oil into a medium sauté pan. Add the artichokes, season with salt and pepper and sauté them over medium high heat for about 10 minutes, shaking the pan to prevent them from sticking. (Test the artichokes by inserting the point of a paring knife into them as they cook. They should be tender enough to allow the knife to slide in without resistance.) If the artichokes still prove to be tough after 10 minutes of cooking, add 2 to 3 tablespoons of water to the pan and continue sautéing and stirring until the artichokes are tender.

Season the langoustines with salt and pepper. Heat 2 tablespoons of the unflavored oil in another pan, and sauté the tails over medium heat, turning them once until they are slightly firm and golden. When the asparagus is cooked, remove from the saucepan with tongs, and place into a water bath to stop the cooking and maintain color. Slice the asparagus into thirds and add to the sauté pan with the artichokes, stirring to combine.

Boil the pasta in the same water you used to cook the asparagus. (Using the asparagus cooking water saves the extra step of heating another pot of boiling water as well as adding flavor to the pasta as it cooks.) The pasta cooks very quickly, in 1 to 2 minutes. It is ready once it floats to the surface of the boiling water and looks somewhat translucent. When the ravioli are cooked, remove them with a large slotted skimmer to a plate or a kitchen towel, working until all the ravioli are ready.

Assemble the ravioli by pouring a small pool of the herbed olive oil in the center of a large plate. Arrange the first ravioli on top of the oil. Add parsley leaves to the asparagus and artichoke mixture and stir to combine. Place a tablespoon of this mixture on top of the ravioli, add 2 langoustine tails. Cover with a second ravioli. Spoon a little herbed olive oil on top, garnish with parsley and serve warm. Yield: 4 servings.  ❖

# A Culinary Impresario Conducts a Revered Kitchen
## *Chef Alain Ducasse*
### LOUIS XV RESTAURANT, MONTE CARLO

"I was born with my feet in foie gras," says one of mankind's most acclaimed chefs. The phrase could become jargon, meaning someone born with cooking talent. But Chef Alain Ducasse isn't joking when HE makes such a statement.

Chef Ducasse grew up on a foie gras farm, a fact that did not make him a culinary "shoe-in." Actually, Alain, now a superstar in the history of gastronomy, worked his way up, training under classical chefs before he became known to the world for his innovative Italo-Provençal cooking. Early in his career, he boldly called noted Swiss chef Michel Guerard in search of a job at Eugenie les Bains. Guerard was unenthusiastic. Undaunted, Alain offered to work for free.

His talents were immediately recognized and ironically, he ended up preparing most of the food for Guerard's book, *Cuisine Minceur*.

Alain later worked under such chefs as Roger Verge of Mougins de Moulins in Provence and famous French pastry chef Gaston Lenotre. Now, Alain is a global marvel

as he works in his Escoffier kitchen – the size of three tennis courts – at the Hotel de Paris. His work has been likened to that of a surgeon's – serious and methodical. The chef's menu even contains poetry he pens. "I enjoy writing about my dishes because I want people to understand how they were prepared," he explains.

Abundance and variety of natural resources plus orchards, vineyards, and livestock farms have made Alsace an area of gastronomic significance for centuries. It is fitting that this celebrated chef works here. He will go down in its history as a forerunner and trendsetter, who has earned three Michelin stars and the reverence of the global food community.

Today, what lies beneath his feet is not foie gras. (That's on his stove top now and sometimes with black truffles.) Instead, he stands above the hotel's centuries-old wine cellar. The restaurant is home to somewhere between 500,000 and 700,000 wine bottles as well as a carafe full of legacy in which the work of Chef Alain Ducasse will ever be embedded. ❖

# Roasted Red Snapper with Herbs and Lemons in an Onion Sauce

*The sweetness of the onions mixed with the fresh-cleanse of the fennel
is only part of the wonderful contrast of ingredients for the snapper.*

## Onion sauce:

1/2 cup extra virgin olive oil

8 large spring onions with 1-inch bulbs, greens removed and cut into 2-3 inch lengths

1/2 cup fish stock or 1 part clam juice mixed with 1 part water
Salt

## Assembly:

8 pieces dried wild fennel sticks, fresh fennel thinly sliced, or omit ingredient

1 lemon, thinly sliced

2 medium, fresh tomatoes

4 whole red snappers, cleaned and scaled (about 1 pound each, or a total of 4 pounds of snapper)

4 teaspoons butter

1/4 cup imported black olives

1/3 cup basil leaves

1 cup fish stock or substitute purchased fish stock or 1 part clam juice and 1 part water

## Onion sauce completion:

1/2 cup small imported black olives
Juice of one half of a lemon

1/2 cup basil leaves, cut chiffonade-style

Preheat oven to 450 degrees°.

Make the onion sauce to serve as an accompaniment to the snapper by adding 2 tablespoons of olive oil to a hot sauté pan. Add the spring onion bulbs and the onion greens and sauté over high heat for 1 minute. Add 1/4 cup of the fish stock, bring it to a boil, season to taste with salt, reduce the heat and cover the pan. Simmer the onions over low heat for about 4 minutes or until they are just tender.

While the onions are cooking, choose an oval, nonreactive baking dish large enough to hold all the fish. Pour 2 tablespoons of olive oil into the dish and spread it around with your fingers. Scatter the bottom of the dish with the fennel sticks. Thinly slice a lemon and arrange it on the bottom of the casserole. Add the tomatoes.

Salt the snapper inside and out and place into the baking dish. Add one teaspoon of butter to each fish. Scatter the olives and basil over them and pour in the 1 cup of fish stock. Add a final drizzle of olive oil before putting fish in the oven. To prevent the fish from over-browning, place a sheet of aluminum foil over the baking dish.

After the onions have simmered for about 4 minutes, add the black olives, 1 tablespoon olive

*(continued)*

# Wine Suggestion

**Simi Chardonnay.** Layers of complex concentrated fruit and a creamy silken texture will result in an integration of flavors when served with this delectable roasted red snapper.

49

oil, and the remaining stock. Reduce the heat, cover the pan and continue to simmer for about 2 more minutes.

Bake the fish for approximately 10 minutes, or until the flesh is firm, yet tender, and yields slightly to the pressure of your finger. (The general rule for cooking fish is 10 minutes for each inch of thickness at 450°.)

Remove the fish from the oven and pour the juices that have accumulated around it into a sauce pan. Add the lemon juice, one tablespoon of olive oil, salt to taste, and the chiffonade of fresh basil. (Chiffonade means to slice herbs or greens into thin strips. To chiffonade, roll the leaves together tightly and slice crosswise.) Serve the fish in the baking dish, pour the lemon-herb fish juices and the onion sauce into separate sauce boats and serve. Yield: 4 servings. ❖

*Fennel grows in a bulb shape like celery. It is a naturally sweet vegetable with an anise or licorice flavor. It becomes sweeter as it cooks, even without the addition of sugar. Dried wild fennel sticks serve as a flavoring agent in a recipe. They grow along roadsides in Mediterranean countries and in California, and have a more pungent taste and aroma than the cultivated variety.*

# Asparagus with Morel Mushrooms in Asparagus-and-Cream Purée

*Fresh asparagus spears with mushrooms are draped with a sauce of asparagus purée and whipped cream.*

2 pounds fresh asparagus, woody ends snapped and lower stems, peeled

Salt

12 ounces fresh morel mushrooms (or 6 ounces dried) or dried shiitake, chanterelles, or porcini

2 shallots, chopped

4 tablespoons extra virgin olive oil

3 tablespoons butter

2 garlic cloves, minced

6 tablespoons chicken stock

1 ounce Parmesan cheese

3 tablespoons whipped cream

Juice of one half of a lemon

Cook the asparagus in boiling, salted water until al dente. While the asparagus are cooking, trim the stems from the morels and cut them in half lengthwise. Wash the fresh morels in a pan of water, changing the water several times until it runs clear. Drain the morels in a sieve. If using dried, soak in warm water until softened (about 30 minutes). Peel and mince the shallots.

Heat 2 tablespoons of the oil and 1 tablespoon of butter in a small saucepan until it sizzles. Add the morels, the garlic, and the shallots. Stir the mixture and season to taste with salt.

Add 6 tablespoons of chicken stock. Bring to a boil. Cover and simmer for 10 to 12 minutes or until the morels are tender.

To make the asparagus purée, remove the asparagus spears from the boiling water and immediately stop the cooking by plunging them into a cold water bath. When cool, cut off about 2 inches from the bottom of the asparagus stalks. Put these pieces into a fine sieve, placed in a bowl, and press them with the back of a spoon against the mesh, extracting the pulp. Use a pastry scraper or a spatula to scrape off the asparagus purée from the sieve. Set this aside for a moment.

Add 2 tablespoons of the olive oil and 2 tablespoons of the butter to a saucepan. When the butter sizzles, add the asparagus. Meanwhile, check the

*(continued)*

mushrooms and drain the accumulated juices from them into a clean saucepan to warm. Add the asparagus purée to the mushroom juices.

Add the Parmesan cheese to the asparagus and sauté briefly, watching closely so as not to overcook the asparagus. When the asparagus are lightly browned, arrange them on individual plates. Arrange the morels on top of the asparagus. Spoon the remaining olive oil/butter combination over the asparagus. Whisk the whipped cream into the reserved asparagus purée and mushroom juices, and heat through. Complete the sauce by squeezing a lemon over the finished dish. Yield: 4 servings ❖

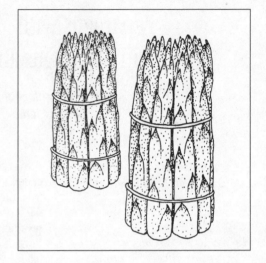

*The Bordeaux region of France makes some of the world's most wonderful red wines — rich, robust and complex. When looking for a similar type of wine from a different growing area, choose one that is labeled Cabernet Sauvignon, Cabernet Franc, or Merlot, three of the traditional varietals used to create most Bordeaux. Some wineries blend all three grapes to make a wine that is in the style of a Bordeaux. Others may choose to use only one grape.*

# A Chef's Garden Blooms with Provençal Aroma

## *Chef Jean-Claude Guillon*

### HOTEL BEL-AIR CAP-FERRAT, CÔTE D'AZUR

The Mediterranean Sea ripples merrily onto the silken sand by the Hotel Bel-Air Cap-Ferrat, setting the mood for guests of the outdoor café. Diners repose in enjoyment of the region's natural beauty – and the intimate and exquisite hotel's renowned flavor.

Chef Jean-Claude Guillon has been at the hotel for some 22 years, leaving only in winter when the Bel-Air closes and the renowned chef travels through Europe, teaching promising culinary students. You might say Chef Guillon was born with a whisk in hand. Early on he was surrounded by a grandmother who cooked for noblemen in a castle and a mother who owned a restaurant. He began formal training at thirteen and studied and worked in Strasbourg, Cannes, and Provence. Even during his stint in the navy, the young chef was appointed the admiral's private cook.

Today, the chef is quick to applaud his kitchen crew. "They are like a soccer team," he describes. The chef is "captain" and his staff members are the players – working to achieve the same goal.

Traditional dishes such as the recipe here for Rack of Lamb à la Provençal, and strawberry desserts are made with ingredients that stem from the chef's bountiful seven-acre garden, just outside the kitchen door. Chef Guillon, like his garden full of local tastes, always has something fresh and fragrant to offer his guests. ❖

# Rack of Lamb à la Provençal

*Prepared with the spices and herbs of the provinces, this lamb recipe includes vegetables and potatoes for a complete and favorful meal.*

## Wine Suggestion

**Ruffino Cabreo Il Borgo.** Cabernet Sauvignon grapes are blended with the traditional Sangiovese to yield flavorful wine that is ideal with lamb.

2   racks of lamb, well-trimmed (about 2 $^1/_2$ to 3 pounds)

Salt and freshly ground pepper

3   teaspoons herbs de Provence (or 2 tablespoons chopped fresh parsley)

$^3/_4$   cup olive oil

4   large white potatoes, pre-cooked, skins removed

4   tablespoons butter

12   ripe cherry tomatoes, cut in half and stems and seeds removed

$^1/_2$   cup fresh bread crumbs

$^1/_4$   cup chopped parsley

2   cloves minced garlic

12   large white mushrooms, cleaned

$^1/_2$   cup concentrated lamb, veal or beef stock (optional)

Begin by seasoning the rack of lamb to taste with salt, pepper and some of the herbs de Provence. Pour 2 tablespoons of the olive oil into a large skillet and heat it until it is quite hot. Position the racks of lamb in the pan, fat-side down (to protect the meat and keep it moist). Sauté for 2 to 3 minutes, or until the lamb forms a brown crust. Preheat the oven to 475°.

Meanwhile, trim the ends and sides of the potatoes, squaring them. Slice into a large dice. Check the lamb and turn the racks, browning them on the other side. Bake in the oven in the sauté pan or a roasting pan for about 12 minutes or until the lamb is medium rare. (Juices will run.)

While the lamb is roasting, prepare the tomatoes and potatoes. Heat 2 tablespoons of the olive oil and of the butter in a medium skillet. Add the potatoes to the hot butter and oil, and shake and sauté them for 4 to 5 minutes over medium heat or until they are crusty and golden. Remove them from the pan, drain on paper towels and set them aside. Reserve the pan as is for later use.

Pour 2 tablespoons of the oil into another skillet. Add the tomatoes, cut-side up, and season them to taste with salt and pepper. Sauté the tomatoes over medium heat for 1 to 2 minutes, and then add them to the lamb to roast in the oven for about 5 minutes.

Combine the bread crumbs, parsley, garlic, remaining herbs de Provence, and salt and pepper to taste in a medium bowl. Remove the tomatoes and sprinkle them with about 2 tablespoons of this mixture, and 2 tablespoons of the olive oil. Return them to the oven.

Quarter the mushrooms. Heat 2 tablespoons of the olive oil and the remaining butter in a medium skillet over high heat. Add the mushrooms to the pan. Add salt to taste, and sauté mushrooms for 2 to 3 minutes or until lightly browned.

Pour the prepared concentrated lamb stock into a saucepan to heat. Remove the lamb from the oven, and sprinkle each rack with about 1 tablespoon of the bread crumb mixture. Drizzle the remaining olive oil over the top. Return the potatoes to the pan. Season

with salt and toss with the remaining bread crumb mixture, the potatoes, and sautéed mushrooms.

Put the racks of lamb on a serving platter. Arrange the mushrooms, tomatoes, and potatoes in piles around the meat. Serve the warm lamb stock in a sauce boat with the lamb. Yield: Makes 4 servings. ❖

*Racks and chops are prepared by butchers in France by trimming away all fat and meat from the lower protruding bone. They call this method frenching.*

*Herbs de Provence is a dried combination of the fresh herbs most commonly used in the south of France — basil, thyme, rosemary, lavender, fennel seed, sage, marjoram, and summer savory. Here, bouquets of herbs de Provence are found at gourmets shops in small clay pots.*

# Crispy Wild Strawberry Cake

*It is easy to see why this dessert could also be called a sundae.*
*It is fluffed high with layers of berries, cookies and whipped cream.*

**Pastry cream:**

  2  *cups milk*
  1  *cup granulated sugar plus*
      *1 tablespoon*
  4  *eggs*
  ¼  *cup cornstarch*
  2  *vanilla beans, halved and*
      *seeds scraped away*

**Crispy cookies:**

  1  *cup chopped almonds*
  ½  *cup all-purpose flour*
  1  *cup confectioners' sugar*
  2  *tablespoons butter*
  1  *tablespoon orange zest*
  ¼  *cup orange juice*
  6  *tablespoons Grand Marnier*

**Assembly:**

  1  *cup heavy cream, whipped*
  2  *pints wild strawberries or*
      *raspberries, plus 4 for*
      *garnish*
  1  *cup strawberry purée*
      *(see Fruit Purée recipe on*
      *page 170)*
      *Mint leaves, for garnish*

Prepare the pastry cream by pouring the milk into a saucepan. Add 1 tablespoon of the sugar, and warm over medium heat. Separate the eggs, reserving the whites for another recipe. In a medium bowl, add the remaining sugar, the 4 yolks and whisk very well to combine. Add the cornstarch and continue to whisk until the mixture is smooth and blended. Add the vanilla beans.

Pour the warm milk into the egg-sugar mixture and whisk to combine. Pour this mixture back into the saucepan and return to heat. Whisk continuously until it thickens to the consistency of pudding. Remove the pan from the stove. Pour the mixture into a bowl. Whisk slightly and set it aside to cool.

Prepare the crispy cookie. Preheat oven to 425°. In a large mixing bowl, mix together the almonds, flour, ½ cup of the confectioners' sugar, and butter with a spoon until the mixture holds together. Add the orange zest, orange juice, 4 tablespoons of the Grand Marnier and the remaining confectioners' sugar. Mix well. Spoon about 1 tablespoon of the batter out onto a cookie sheet and flatten each cookie with the back of a fork. Bake for 10 minutes or until the cookies are golden but still soft. Remove the baking sheet from the oven and allow the cookies to set and harden a bit before removing them with a spatula.

Mix 3 tablespoons of the pastry cream with 2

Mix 3 tablespoons of the pastry cream with 2 tablespoons of the whipped cream to lighten it and then combine the remaining pastry cream with the remaining whipped cream. Flavor it by sprinkling it with the remaining Grand Marnier.

To serve, place a dollop of the pastry cream/whipped cream mixture in the middle of a large dinner plate and cover it with a cookie, pushing down to flatten slightly. Place another spoonful of the same mixture on top of the cookie, and add some wild strawberries, pushing them into the cream. Place another cookie on top, add a spoonful of the pastry cream/whipped cream mixture, spreading it out with the back of the spoon, and add another layer of berries. Top with another cookie and pour the strawberry purée around the base of the plate in a thin stream. Garnish with a sprig of mint and a wild strawberry. Yield: 4 servings. ❖

*Vanilla pod is the fruit of a tropical lily native to North America. It must be hand pollinated, takes eight to nine months to mature, and then must be cured or fermented over a three-to-six-month period. Most vanilla sold in the United States is vanilla in an alcohol-and-water solution.*

*Grand Marnier is a liquer that was introduced by the Marnier-Lapostolle family firm in 1880.*

# Medieval and Other Ages Inspire Decor and New Dishes
## *Chef Didier Lefeuvre*
### CHÂTEAU D'ISENBOURG, ROUFFACH

Here in this, one of the oldest castles in the Alsace region, you can spend the night in rooms with themes that span the centuries – beneath Medieval armor in one or surrounded by elaborate furnishings from Louis XV's day in another. So too, the influence of cooking styles that date from the Middle Ages and beyond, emerge from the past only to appear – reinterpreted on dining room tables at the Château d'Isenbourg.

"There is an evolution in cooking," suggests Chef Didier Lefeuvre, "and it's away from nouvelle cuisine to more classical dishes." Recipes followed at the château are often remakes of 15th- and 16th-century originals adapted for today. This, coupled with romantic rooms from the past, offers guests the experience of traveling back in time.

"Before, where one ladle of heavy cream was used (in a recipe), now there is one teaspoon," says Didier. He explains that the essence of the dish is retained by beating this smaller amount of cream to make it fluffier.

It has been said of Chef Lefeuvre that he is on the cutting edge of the changing culinary identity of his homeland. As you can see in the lasagne recipe here, the dish is full of flavor but the chef gives it a modern twist by seasoning it with Harissa – a North African spice – plus a hot-pepper sauce, and saffron. Very different, very new, and still uniquely very French for the 20th century. ❖

# Vegetable Lasagne

*Unlike many lasagne recipes, this dish goes easy on the cheese and employs instead a purée of both eggplant and tomatoes and a zucchini-and-cream topping. The recipe calls for having freshly made pasta dough prepared in advance.*

## Wine Suggestion

**Sichel Riesling** is made from Riesling grapes and yields a bone-dry wine with soft almond over-tones that is a fine choice when serving dishes that blend flavorful and fragrant herbs with vegetables and pungent spice. The crisp Sichel Riesling will leave the palate refreshed.

### Eggplant purée:

1 eggplant (about 1 1/4 pounds)
1/4 cup olive oil
    Salt
1/2 cup diced shallots
    Salt and pepper

### Filling:

6 small tomatoes
1/2 cup diced onions
4 cloves garlic
1/2 teaspoon Harissa Sauce, or any hot pepper sauce
1/8 teaspoon saffron threads, optional
1 tablespoon chopped parsley
3 teaspoons chopped thyme
1 bay leaf
3/4 cup diced zucchini (3/4-inch dice)
2 tablespoons dry Vermouth
1/2 pound pasta dough, rolled out to 1/16-inch thick and cut into 2 1/2-inch-wide by 13-inch-long strips to fit a 9x13-inch casserole dish
1/4 cup heavy cream
1/2 cup grated Parmesan cheese

Preheat oven to 400°. Place the whole, unpeeled eggplant on a piece of aluminum foil, shiny-side out. Pour 1 tablespoon of the olive oil and some salt over the entire surface. Wrap the entire eggplant firmly in aluminum foil. Bake on the shelf in the oven for about 40 minutes or until the eggplant is softened. When baked, remove the eggplant from the oven, unwrap and discard the foil. Cut the eggplant in half lengthwise. Remove the flesh by scraping with a spoon. Place into a bowl and set aside.

Make a purée of the eggplant. Heat a skillet or sauté pan over medium heat. Add 1 teaspoon of the olive oil. Add the shallots and sauté until transparent. Add the eggplant and season with salt and pepper. Lower the heat and sauté for about 25 minutes. Remove the cooked eggplant from the pan. While still hot, press the eggplant through a sieve. Set the eggplant purée aside and keep warm.

Bring a medium saucepan of water to the boil. Meanwhile, prepare an ice bath in a bowl with water and ice. Core the tomatoes and cut a cross on the rounded ends. Drop them into the boiling water. Cook for about 45 seconds and quickly plunge into the ice bath. Remove the tomatoes from the ice water and peel, cutting them in half and squeezing gently to remove the seeds and bitter juices. Coarsely chop the tomatoes and set aside. Reserve the cooking water

*(continued)*

from the tomatoes and set on a low flame to keep hot. This water can be used to cook the pasta.

In another skillet, sauté the onions in 1 teaspoon of the olive oil until tender. Add the chopped tomatoes. Sauté the garlic and season with salt, pepper, Harissa sauce, and the saffron. Add the chopped parsley, 2 teaspoons of the thyme, and the bay leaf. Cook the tomatoes over low heat for about 30 minutes, or until a thick tomato purée develops. Set aside.

While the tomatoes are cooking, trim the zucchini and julienne with the skin intact. In another skillet, heat $1/2$ teaspoon olive oil and sauté the zucchini, stirring frequently, cooking until just tender. Season with salt, pepper, and the Vermouth. Set aside.

Make sure the water for the pasta is slightly boiling and salted. Cook the pasta al dente and then plunge into cold water to stop the cooking process. Layer the bottom of a 9x13-inch baking dish with lasagne noodles and spread with the tomato purée. Add another layer of pasta and spread with the reserved eggplant purée. Season with the remaining 1 teaspoon of thyme.

Lightly whip the cream. Fold the sautéed zucchini into the cream to combine. Spread overtop the lasagne. Sprinkle with the Parmesan cheese. Lower the oven heat to 350° and bake the lasagne for 15 minutes or until heated through. Glaze lightly under the broiler just before serving. Let stand for 5 minutes and then cut into individual 4-inch squares. Yield: 4 servings. ❖

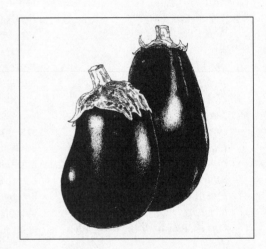

# Foie Gras of Duck with Artichokes

*The fattening of goose or duck to produce enlarged livers as a delicacy goes back to ancient Rome.*
*The tradition continues today with many interesting varieties of foie gras, such as the one here.*

4   large artichokes

1   lemon

   Salt

1/2   cup water

2   tablespoons all-purpose flour

1/4   pound mache leaves or mesclun

1   foie gras of duck (about 1 pound)

   Freshly ground pepper

1   tablespoon dijon-style mustard

3   tablespoons sherry vinegar

3   tablespoons hazelnut oil

2   tablespoons butter

2   tablespoons hazelnuts, skins removed and sliced

2   shallots, peeled and minced

1/2   cup duck, veal, or beef stock

Prepare the artichokes by breaking off the stems, cutting off the base and around the bottom to remove the outer leaves and chopping off the top half to reveal the center core. Trim the artichoke base, removing all the green. Trim off all the excess outer fiber until the center or heart of the artichoke is reached. Discard the artichoke trimmings.

Cut the lemon in half. Rub the artichoke heart with the cut side of the lemon to prevent discoloration. Place artichoke hearts in a small saucepan and cover with water. Salt the water, squeeze the juice of half of the lemon and add it to the pan. Add the reserved artichoke hearts and the other half of the lemon.

Make a blanc by whisking the water into the flour in a small bowl to form a smooth mixture. Whisk the blanc into the saucepan with the artichokes and continue to cook the hearts until they are tender, about 6 to 8 minutes.

Arrange the mache leaves in a circle on a large dinner plate and reserve them in the refrigerator until ready to serve.

While the artichoke hearts are cooking, prepare the foie gras. Separate the small lobe from the foie gras and cut it diagonally, removing 1 slice. Cut 3 more 1/2-inch slices at an angle and score them on 1 side in a cross-hatch diamond pattern. Arrange the foie

*(continued)*

## Wine Suggestion

**Cuvée Dom Pérignon.** A champagne of great stature, named after the Benedictine monk who discovered how to make wine sparkle. The sublime combination of rich buttery foie gras and a fine champagne offers a host of complex flavors and lush textures. Since Dom Pérignon is made from only the finest grapes (Chardonnay and Pinot Noir) and only in the best years, there always will be a vintage stated on the label. Cuvée Dom Pérignon is aged in the bottle for about 7 years.

gras on a plate, season to taste with salt and pepper on both sides, and refrigerate until ready to cook.

Remove the artichoke hearts from the saucepan and place them in the refrigerator to cool.

Prepare a vinaigrette. In a small bowl, whisk together the mustard, 1 tablespoon of the sherry vinegar, and salt and pepper to taste. Whisk in the hazelnut oil.

Remove the chokes from the artichoke hearts and trim off any tough excess. (The choke is the tough inedible center of the artichoke heart.) Turn the hearts over and cut them into pie-shaped wedges, season to taste with salt and pepper, and put about 1 teaspoon of butter on each one. Put them in the oven to keep warm while you cook the foie gras.

Remove the foie gras from the refrigerator. Sauté the slices very briefly in a preheated, nonstick pan, cross-hatch-side down, turning them after about 20 to 30 seconds, once they are brown. Remove them from the pan with a spatula, placing them on a plate. Sprinkle each one with some of the chopped nuts. Put them in the oven to keep warm while you finish the dish.

Sauté the 2 tablespoons of minced shallots in the same pan where you sautéed the foie gras. Deglaze the pan with the remaining sherry vinegar and add $1/4$ cup of duck stock. Reduce the sauce to almost half over high heat and season to taste with salt and pepper. Enrich the sauce with 1 tablespoon of butter, swirling the pan to melt and incorporate. Taste for seasoning. Strain the sauce through a strainer into another saucepan, keeping it warm.

Remove the mache leaves from the refrigerator and the artichoke hearts from the oven. Place an artichoke heart in the center of each circle of mache leaves. Arrange 2 slices of foie gras on top and spoon some of the sauce around the base of the plate. Sprinkle with a few additional nuts and serve warm. Yield: 4 servings. ❖

*Mescluns are baby lettuces made up of a combination of lettuce such as frissée and radicchio.*

# The Day's Catch Becomes the Daily Pride
## *Chef Serge Philippin*
### LE BACON RESTAURANT, ANTIBES

Le Bacon is one of those family restaurants charmingly tied to a philosophy that has made it famous. It all began with fisherman Victor Sordello who purchased land in 1948 and opened Le Bacon so that everyone could enjoy seafood fresh.

In Antibes, local fishermen, arriving back at their piers every morning, are an integral part of the region and make it possible for Le Bacon to continue its proud tradition of serving only the freshest seafood to its customers.

Current owners Adrieu and Etienne Sordello (Victor's sons), who maintain the family practice of serving only the best, rise early and head to the fish market. Later each morning, they confer with Chef Serge Philippin to decide on the menu based on the fish in their sacks.

From Serge's kitchen, guests are served seafood that is only a few hours old. Chef Philippin can almost be called family, as he has been at Le Bacon for 15 years. He earned the restaurant a Michelin star for – among other preparations and methods – serving food in its most natural flavor. The recipe for the fish en papillote or "in parchment," for example, is cooked almost rare to preserve the taste, and the paper helps the fish to steam in its own juices.

When he is not boiling up a bouillabaisse or browning a brulêé, Chef Philippin bicycles about the region with a camera in hand instead of a spatula, only anxious to return to his kitchen again. ❖

# Filet of Flounder en Papillote

*Fish cooked in parchment almost ensures a moist serving of sole and flounder,
and one full of a variety of flavors, such as the combination in this recipe.*

## Wine Suggestion

**Domaine Chandon Brut Cuvée.** A simply prepared fish with a flavorful and lively dry sparkling wine is one of life's great pleasures. Brut indicates that this California sparkler is one of the driest and will be easy to match with food.

1   lemon

2-3   medium plum tomatoes, peeled, seeded, and chopped

3   tablespoons olive oil

$1/8$   teaspoon ginger

   Salt and freshly ground pepper

4   fresh tarragon sprigs

1   tablespoon butter

1   (1 - 1 $1/2$ pound) flounder filet (or sole or John Dory)

   Parchment paper

   Tarragon, as garnish

Preheat the oven to 475°. Cut the lemon in half. Scrape the tomatoes into a small sauce boat and squeeze 1 tablespoon of lemon juice over them. Add the olive oil and ginger. Season to taste. Chop the tarragon finely and add it to the sauce boat. Add the butter and stir to blend.

Make sure that the parchment rectangles are 9 x 13 inches or 2 inches larger in diameter than the fish. Place the fish in the center of one of the rectangles. Season the fish with salt and pepper and cover with the tomato mixture. Place the other sheet of parchment over the fish, making sure the edges meet. Beginning at one corner of the parchment, fold over the edges to form a hem. In a continuous motion, fold the entire fish into the parchment with a single hem. Again, beginning in a corner, roll the hem over and press down firmly to press the seal together lightly. (If parchment paper is unavailable, use un-waxed freezer paper.)

Oil the baking sheet and slide the parchment onto it. Bake the fish for about 15 minutes or until the parchment paper is puffed and golden and the fish is tender.

Slit open the parchment, scrape the tomato mixture to the side. Remove the skin from the fish and lift off $1/2$ of the filet. Lift off the other filet. Remove the center bone, scrape off the skin from the remaining filet and put it onto the plate, reconstructing the shape of the fish. Arrange some of the tomatoes on the plate and spoon the accumulated juices around the fish. Spoon 2 teaspoons of the reserved tomato mixture over the filets, garnish with tarragon and serve the fish warm. Yield: 4 servings. ❖

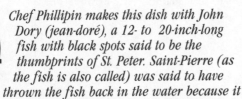

*Chef Phillipin makes this dish with John Dory (jean-doré), a 12- to 20-inch-long fish with black spots said to be the thumbprints of St. Peter. Saint-Pierre (as the fish is also called) was said to have thrown the fish back in the water because it was moaning (which it does when removed from water). Tradition also has it that the apostle took a coin from the fish's mouth on Jesus' instruction.*

# Bouillabaisse

*There are many versions of this recipe, but the thread that holds them together
is the basic combination of fish boiled with herbs, olive oil, and spices.*

## Wine Suggestion

**Moët & Chandon Brut Impérial.** A brut champagne with fish and shellfish is a meal fit for a king. In fact, Louis XIV, a lover of the bubbly, and most of his successors, served champagne with a variety of dishes, including fish.

**Bouillabaisse broth:**

- ¼  cup olive oil
- 1  medium onion, coarsely chopped
- 1  bulb unpeeled garlic, cut in half horizontally
- 1  tablespoon tomato paste
- 1  medium branch celery
- 2  small ripe tomatoes, cut in quarters

**Fish for the Bouillabaisse broth:**

- 7-8  pounds, small, whole cleaned fish such as John Dory, Rascasse, Vives, Grondin, and Baudroie. Substitute: red mullet, sea bass, rockfish or red snapper
- 2  laurel leaves
- 1  bunch dry wild fennel sticks or 2 branches fresh fennel
- 1  small bunch fresh thyme
    Salt
- 4  cups boiling water
- 4  teaspoons saffron

**Fish for the Bouillabaisse:**

- 8  pounds medium fish such as red snapper, rockfish, sea bass and monkfish or shellfish such as shrimp, mussels or clams

**Sauce Rouille:**

- 4 - 6  cloves garlic
- 2  teaspoons cayenne pepper
- 2  egg yolks
    Salt

- ½  cup olive oil
- 4-6  teaspoons tomato paste
- 6  toasted bread rounds or more (about ½ -inch thick)

**Assembly:**

- 2  potatoes, boiled and sliced

Pour ¼ cup olive oil into a large soup casserole. Add the chopped onion and stir to coat with oil. Add the garlic halves, and stir and sauté until clear and fragrant. Add the tomato paste and stir to thoroughly coat the garlic and onion. Add the celery, the tomatoes and stir to coat. Stir in the fish, coating them well with the vegetables and oil. Add the laurel, the fennel, the thyme and stir to coat with the oil.  Add salt to taste and 3 cups of the boiling water. Submerge the fish, herbs, and vegetables in the water with a wooden spoon. Add the remaining cup of water and again submerge the solids into the liquid. Cook the fish and broth over high heat until the mixture starts to boil. Add 2 teaspoons of the saffron and again submerge the ingredients. Cook the fish, the vegetables and herbs on a gentle boil long enough so they give their flavor to the broth, about 15 minutes. If necessary, add only enough water to barely cover the ingredients, so the broth will be flavorful and yet there will

*(continued)*

be enough liquid to cook the ingredients.

Remove the fennel stalks and thyme from the soup base after it has boiled about 15 minutes. Place a food mill in a large saucepan and move it to the work surface. (A food mill purées and separates foods at the same time; it works differently from a food processor which only purées or processes without removing the bones.) Lift the soup casserole off the heat and ladle 3 or 4 cups of fish broth and fish into the food mill. Pass the fish through the mill, turning it in opposite directions to extract as much flavor as possible from the vegetables and fish, but eliminating the fish bones and vegetable fibers. Repeat the process with the remaining soup base. Scrape the base of the mill to remove the puréed fish and vegetables clinging to it.

Strain the liquid through another finer sieve using a wooden pestle or spoon to push the liquid and solids against the mesh of the sieve. Rinse out the casserole you have used to prepare the broth for the bouillabaisse. Pour the fish broth back into it and heat it over medium heat. Add the "fish for bouillabaisse" to the broth. Mix in 2 teaspoons of saffron. Simmer the fish until they are opaque but not falling apart, submerging them in the liquid until they are done.

Prepare the rouille. Place the garlic, pepper, egg yolks, and a little salt in a blender or processor and whirl until smooth. Pour in the olive oil, slowly so that the sauce thickens and becomes creamy; if the oil is added too quickly, the mixture will separate. At this point, the tomato paste can be added and very quickly blended to a smooth paste. Add the cayenne. Spread rouille onto toasted bread rounds.

Remove the fish from the soup casserole and place on a serving dish. At the table, filet the fish and place a filet of each fish in a large flat soup tureen. Place some sliced potato on the fish and a few toasted bread rounds, which you have spread with rouille. Finally, pour the hot soup into the tureen and serve the bouillabaisse immediately. Yield: 6 servings. ❖

*Bouillabaisse was originally cooked on the beach by fishermen, who used a large cauldron over a wood fire to cook the fish least suitable for market.*

❖

*Saffron is a pungent, aromatic spice and one of the world's most expensive. It is used to flavor and tint food. Coming from the stigmas of a small purple crocus, it takes 14,000 of these crocuses to make just one ounce of saffron — but small amounts do go a long way.*

# A Bouquet of Nations Graces His Table
## *Chef Arnaud Poëtte*
### EDEN ROC AT HOTEL DU CAP, ANTIBES

The recipe for Mediterranean Sea Bass that Chef Poëtte has provided here, has been a part of this famous restaurant's menu for some fifteen years, as one of its most requested dishes. Serving it at home will literally enliven the dining table with the taste of the Mediterranean and the techniques of a very special chef.

Chef Arnaud Poëtte has trained in some of the most celebrated kitchens, including some in Switzerland, Tokyo, and Dublin. He picks the best of the culinary buds and blooms – the hallmark ingredients from a variety of cultures – in designing his ever-evolving repertoire. Since 1983, he has been at the hotel in many positions from chef de partie to sous chef. Now, as head chef, he serves the most discriminating at this luxurious retreat.

This chef is accustomed to serving heads of state and preparing the cuisine for international summits. They all applaud him, for his food is sincerely fresh, containing only those ingredients that are currently growing under the Mediterranean sun.

"We are losing the concept of season," suggests Chef Poëtte. "We eat watermelon all year. I strive for using the fruits of local production." He also buys his herbs fresh – from a friend who tends a private garden without any chemical pesticides. Herbs are purchased fresh daily and sometimes personally selected by the chef himself, who enjoys hand-picking his ingredients. And in Cap Antibes, there are many of these small-scale producers who are large contributors to the marvelous, memorable menus for which Arnaud Poëtte has become so well-known. ❖

# Mushroom-Stuffed Mediterranean Sea Bass with Wild Fennel and Beurre Blanc

*More than one cooking preparation is in this recipe, including a white sauce and a mushroom duxelle (mushrooms, onions, and shallots sautéed in butter).*

## Wine Suggestion

**Simi Chardonnay Reserve** can easily be paired with a fish course that contains butter, cream, and herbs, or with any rich foods that call for a cream sauce.

2  sea bass, about 1 ³/₄ pounds each
6  to 8 dried wild fennel sticks or
   fennel seeds to cover the pan,
   or this ingredient is optional
2  tablespoons olive oil

**Flavoring for stuffing:**
4  tomatoes
¹/₄  cup olive oil
3  shallots, minced
1  medium onion, peeled and
   finely chopped
   Salt and freshly ground pepper

**Flavoring for beurre blanc:**
¹/₄  cup olive oil
1  shallot, minced
1  teaspoon herbs de Provence
2  tomatoes, peeled, seeded and
   chopped

**Mushroom Duxelle:**
1  pound button mushrooms
2  tablespoons oil
1  teaspoon herbs de Provence

**Basil mayonnaise:**
1  cup (see pantry recipe, page 156)

**Beurre blanc:**
3  shallots, minced
¹/₂  cup white wine
¹/₄  cup heavy cream
¹/₄  pound butter
   Salt and pepper
8  basil leaves

Bone the sea bass by cutting down along the backbone, separating it from the filets. Detach the central backbone by cutting through it at the head and at the tail and lifting it out. Trim the interior of the fish and wash it under running water until it is clean and ready for stuffing.

Remove the pin bones from the filets with tweezers. (Pin bones can be found in the filets of all round fish. They are a part of the backbone which extends to the filets. You can also use needle-nose pliers and a paring knife to remove the bones.)

Place the dried fennel sticks on the base of a baking dish large enough to hold the fish. This serves as a sort of baking rack. Sprinkle with 2 tablespoons of oil and place the sea bass on top. Open up the back of the fish and ready them for stuffing. Refrigerate the fish.

Meanwhile, prepare the flavoring for the stuffing by making a tomato concassée. Stem the tomatoes and score the base with an X to facilitate peeling the tomato after it is parboiled. Bring a medium saucepan of water to a boil, transfer the tomatoes to the water and parboil them for about 20 seconds or until the peel begins to curl back. Plunge the tomatoes in a cold water bath to stop the cooking. When the tomatoes are cool enough to handle, peel them. Cut off the pulp, leaving the seedy core. Scrape off the seeds with your fingers. Chop the tomatoes in a small dice by placing the flat side of the tomato on the cutting board, cutting each tomato first vertically, then across.

Pour 2 tablespoons of the oil into a medium sauté pan or skillet. Add the shallots and the onion and sauté for about 4 minutes, stirring continually or until clear. Add the tomatoes, season to taste with salt and pepper, and stir to combine. Cook this mixture for 10 to 15 minutes over medium heat or until all the liquid has evaporated and the mixture is thick and dry.

Prepare the flavoring for the beurre blanc or white butter sauce while the tomatoes are cooking. Pour the oil into a medium saucepan, heat the oil until it is very hot, and add $^2/_3$ of the shallots, stirring to combine. Add the herbs de Provence and the tomatoes. Remove the pan from the heat. Set aside. Preheat the oven to 400°.

Continue making the stuffing for the fish by preparing mushroom duxelle. Trim the mushrooms, wash, slice, and chop them. Put them into a food processor and process until finely minced. Pour 2 tablespoons of oil into a medium sauté pan. Add the remaining chopped shallots from the beurre blanc flavoring, to the pan and sauté it for about 1 minute, stirring continually. Add the mushrooms to the pan, season with the herbs de Provence, and salt and pepper to taste. Continue sautéing for about 4 minutes, stirring frequently, or until all the excess liquid has evaporated.

Transfer the duxelle mixture to a medium bowl. Add the sautéed tomato and shallot mixture, and season to taste with salt and pepper. Remove the fish from the refrigerator and season with salt and pepper. Brush the inside of the fish with the basil mayonnaise, using a pastry brush to spread it evenly. Spoon 3 rounded tablespoons of stuffing down the center of the fish. Bake for 20 minutes or until the fish is opaque but still moist.

While the fish is baking, prepare the white butter or beurre blanc. Add the shallots to a medium, nonreactive saucepan and pour in the wine.

Reduce the wine until it is $^1/_2$ of its original volume. Add the cream and whisk in the butter, 1 tablespoon at a time, adding each piece of butter just as the one in the pan melts. Season to taste with salt and pepper. Strain the sauce through a sieve into a medium bowl to remove the shallots. Add 3 tablespoons of the reserved tomato-shallot-and-olive-oil mixture, reserving the rest for another use. Add the basil leaves to the sauce and stir to combine.

Remove the fish from the oven and present it in the baking dish with the basil and tomato-flavored beurre blanc. Yield: 4 servings. ❖

*Duxelle is a mushroom-and-onion mixture used in the preparation of stuffing, sauces, and other dishes.*

# Banana Blinis with Strawberry Purée

*This dessert is a play upon the concept of a blini. Chef Poëtte actually makes a clafouti batter (Clafouti is a French dessert where fruit is covered with a crêpe or pancake-like batter.) He pours it into small round molds so it resembles a blini. A blini is a Russian buckwheat pancake raised with yeast and traditionally served with sour cream and caviar.*

## Wine Suggestion

**Sichel Eiswein.**
This unique dessert wine is made from overripe grapes that have been picked and pressed when still frozen. Eiswein (ice wine) is extremely rare, since Mother Nature must first allow for full ripeness and then attack the grapes with a sudden severe frost. The result is a combination of lively acidity and an intensity of sweetness and flavor.

7   eggs, separated

1¼   cups sugar

1   cup all-purpose flour

2   cups milk

1   stick butter, softened

5   medium bananas

1   pint strawberries

2   tablespoons heavy cream

6   whole strawberries, for garnish

Mint leaves, for garnish

Make the blinis. Whisk the yolks with ¾ cup of the sugar, until the sugar is dissolved and the color turns lemon yellow. Add the flour to the eggs in two stages, ½ cup at a time, whisking to combine. Gradually add the milk, whisking all the time to ensure there are no lumps in the batter.

Preheat the oven to 425°. Use a pastry brush to spread about 1 tablespoon of the softened butter on nonstick pastry molds. Dust them with 1 tablespoon of the sugar. (Use 1 x 4-inch nonstick pastry molds to make these blinis. If you cannot find these, substitute 4-inch ceramic or glass ramekins.) Peel the bananas and cut them at an angle into ¼-inch slices. Melt the remaining butter in a sauté pan and sauté the bananas in stages, for about 30 seconds per side or until golden brown. Remove them from the pan, reserving them on a plate until all are done. Line the bottom of the molds with the sliced bananas, arranging them so they overlap slightly.

Beat the egg whites until they form soft peaks. Add the whites to the blini batter, folding them in gently. Spoon about 2 to 3 tablespoons of the batter into the ramekins or pastry molds until you have about 1 inch of batter in each mold. (It is important not to overfill the molds as the blinis will become more like a soufflé, puff up too much, and won't unmold properly.)

Bake the blinis in the oven for 12 minutes or until they are slightly puffed and golden.

Make the strawberry purée. Remove the stems from the strawberries and cut them in quarters. Put them into a food processor or blender. Add the remaining sugar and purée.

To serve, unmold each blini, fruit-side up, in the center of a large dinner plate. Spoon the strawberry purée around the blini in a half circle. Add 4 drops of heavy cream to the purée and draw a knife through the cream to form a decorative pattern. Cut a whole strawberry vertically and put it on the plate,

rounded-side up. Garnish with mint leaves. Yield: 6 servings. ❖

# Getting Down-to-Earth with Intuitive Dishes

## *Chef Jean-Michel Lorain*

LA CÔTE SAINT-JACQUES, JOIGNY

*"You don't think.*

*You cook."*

*– Lorain*

If there is one way to describe the approach Chef Jean-Michel Lorain takes to food preparation, it is au natural. A recipient of three stars from Michelin early in his career, Jean-Michel creates winning combinations with the "simplest" ingredients. His approach to cooking is non-analytical, tending to freestyle, based on intuition.

"You don't think," observes the chef. "You cook." He enjoys adapting old recipes and combining only two or three tastes into one dish. "I mix the flavors together so all the tastes together – make a good plate," he adds. But oh, are those flavors ever special. The duck breast recipe, which features a coffee-infused sauce made with crushed beans and caramelized endive is such a glorious fusion.

Jean-Michel was a teenager when he decided to follow in his father's footsteps and work in the family restaurant and inn. The chef was influenced by his father's skills in the kitchen and today still relies on his family's opinions (his mother is wine master at La Côte Saint-Jacques). When he experiments with a new dish, the family palates become the testing grounds. "They are very hard on me," Chef Lorain laughs. But he seriously listens to their critique and feels that his willingness to make considerations is why his food is so heralded. ❖

72

# Roasted Duck Breast with Braised Endive in a Crushed-Coffee-Bean Sauce

*Chef Lorain shows his creativity by adding the coffee-bean sauce and the caramelized-and-braised endive to this dish. You may want to prepare the endive before starting the recipe.*

4   *duck breasts, cut in half, skin intact*

*Salt and freshly ground pepper*

2   *tablespoons peanut oil*

1   *lemon*

1   *cup water*

4   *teaspoons sugar*

3   *tablespoons Arabica (or any other strong) coffee beans, crushed*

2   *cups duck broth*

1   *tablespoon butter*

2   *teaspoons extra virgin olive oil*

4   *Belgian endives, caramelized and braised (See Pantry Recipe on Page 169)*

4   *sprigs of flat-leaf parsley*

Season the duck breasts to taste with salt and a few grinds of the pepper. Heat the peanut oil in a sauté pan or skillet over high heat. Add the duck breasts, skin-side down, to the hot pan; sear for 30 seconds. Reduce the heat so that they continue to sauté, sealing in the juices for about five minutes. Check the breasts for brownness. Pour the accumulated juices and fat into another saucepan and turn the breasts over.

While the duck breasts continue to sauté, peel strips from the lemon. Stack the strips of lemon peel and slice them lengthwise julienne style. Blanch lemon peel in a small saucepan containing $1/2$ cup water. (Lemon peel is blanched or boiled briefly in water to remove some of the surface oils and to soften it.)

Check the duck breasts again, testing for doneness by feeling the texture of the meat. It should be medium rare inside and quite springy to the touch.

After blanching the lemon peel for 2 minutes, drain water, and return it to the saucepan to candy the lemon. Prepare it for use as a garnish. Add 2 tablespoons water. Return the pan to the stove. Add the sugar and cook for 5 minutes over low heat.

Check the duck again and remove each breast individually as it tests done. The total cooking time should be about 10 minutes.

Remove the duck breasts from the pan. Discard the accumulated fat and juices and pour in 1 cup water

*(continued)*

# Wine Suggestion

**Marqués de Riscal Baron de Chirel.** Game meats and robust red wines were meant for each other. This wine from the Rioja region of Spain blends the traditional Tempranillo grape with Cabernet Sauvignon, to produce a range of flavors that will stand-up to the intensity of the concentrated sauce.

73

to deglaze the pan. Bring the deglazing liquid to a boil and add the duck broth or chicken stock. Shake the pan to mix the liquids and move the pan off the heat. Add the crushed coffee beans to the duck stock and shake to stir.

Infuse the coffee beans in the sauce for 10 minutes. (Infusion is similar to steeping tea leaves in hot water to make tea. It extracts the flavor from the coffee beans into the duck sauce.) Strain the coffee sauce into a small saucepan using a chinois or a fine strainer or coffee filter. Add the butter, swirling the pan to incorporate it into the sauce.

Add the olive oil to another sauté pan and place it on high heat. Quickly reheat the duck breasts for about 1 minute. Transfer them to a cutting board and remove the skin. Cut the breasts on an angle into 1-inch slices.

To serve, remove the base of the braised and caramelized Belgian endive and fan it out on a dinner plate. Arrange the sliced duck in a similar fan shape on the opposite side of the plate and garnish with the lemon peel. Whisk the coffee sauce briefly and spoon it on the plate. Garnish with a sprig of parsley. Yield: 4 servings. ❖

 *Deglazing the pan is a technique used to loosen the bits of browned food and juices that adhere to the bottom of the pan. These juices are "lifted" out of the pan by the addition of a liquid (such as a wine or water) and become the basis for a sauce.*

*Belgian endive is a dish that represents its origins very well. It is found almost everywhere in the Brussels region and is very popular. Interest-ingly, it is grown in complete darkness to prevent it from turning green.*

# Petite Crêpes with Grapefruit Sauce

*Refreshing and delicious, this light dessert is a winning palate pleaser.*

## Wine Suggestion

**Sichel Beerenauslese.** Beerenauslese (selectively harvested overripe grapes) from Germany yields sublime flavors that dance on the palate and are reminiscent of ripe pear, peaches, citrus fruits, and honey.

### Crêpe batter:
- 1  egg yolk
- 2  whole eggs
- 4  tablespoons sugar
- 1/2  cup all-purpose flour
- 1/8  teaspoon salt
- 1  cup milk
- 2  tablespoons butter, melted and cooled to room temperature

### Candied grapefruit peel:
- 2  large grapefruits, peeled with a potato peeler. Use only 3 large strips of peel, reserving the rest for another recipe. Set grapefruit aside for the sauce.
- 1  teaspoon sugar
- 2  tablespoons water

### Grapefruit sauce:
- Juice of the reserved grapefruit to equal 1 cup
- 1  large grapefruit, peeled and sliced into segments (peel reserved)
- 1/2  cup sugar
- 2  tablespoons water

### Assembly:
- Crêpes
- Candied grapefruit peel
- Grapefruit sections
- 1  pint lemon sorbet
- Fresh mint for garnish

Prepare the crêpe batter. In a medium bowl, place the egg yolk and whole eggs. Gradually whisk in the sugar and add the flour, 1/4 cup at a time. Add the salt and continue to whisk. Add the milk, 1/2 cup at a time. Continue to mix thoroughly. Add the butter and whisk to blend thoroughly. Let the batter rest in the refrigerator for at least 1 hour before use. (This produces a thinner, more pliable crêpe that does not stick to the pan as easily.)

Prepare the candied grapefruit. Separate the strips of the grapefruit peel and place them into a saucepan over medium-high heat with the sugar and water. Blanch for about 10 minutes or until the liquid has reduced and the strips have formed a candied coating. Remove from the heat and set aside.

To prepare the sauce, pour the grapefruit juice into a saucepan. Add the sugar and whisk to combine. Cook over medium-high heat for about 10 minutes or until the sauce is reduced. (The sauce will be runny.)

Prepare to cook the crêpes. Brush butter on the inside of an 8-inch, nonstick pan and place it on the stove to heat.

To test the temperature of the pan, flick a few drops of the batter into the pan. When the drops of batter brown quickly at the edges, the

*(continued)*

75

pan is ready. Add about 2 tablespoons of batter to the heated pan and rotate the pan to spread the batter thinly and evenly. Cook the crêpe until the batter on top is set and the bottom is brown. Flip the crêpe over to cook on the other side. Repeat this process until all of the batter is used.

After all of the crêpes have been cooked, begin assembly. First place a very small amount of the candied peel into the center of each crêpe. Then fold the crêpe in half horizontally. Fold in half again to form a triangle.

After all of the crêpes have been folded, place 3 on each plate, slightly overlapping the corners. Arrange a few strips of the candied peel and 4 of the grapefruit sections onto the top of the crêpes. Spoon 2 rounded table-spoons of lemon sorbet in the center and garnish with fresh -mint and a spoon of the grape-fruit sauce. Yield: 4 servings. ❖

*Braising is a cooking method that applies slow, moist heat. It is used for heartier vegetables and tougher cuts of meat. The vegetables are cooked in butter or oil and a liquid is added. A cover, such as aluminum foil is added to retain moisture.*

# A Culinary Impressionist "Paints" Paris
## *Chef Emile Tabourdiau*
### HOTEL LE BRISTOL, PARIS

The great French Impressionist painter Pierre Auguste Renoir had a knack for filling a canvas with piquant touches and vivacious poses. Well, one cannot help but make the comparison here, as Chef Emile Tabourdiau's artwork on the plate is enlivened with color, form, and taste. His artistry, while of a different palette, is created with passion and something new and inviting in every culinary stroke.

Perhaps what the chef learns from his routine studies of fine art paintings has spilled over into the kitchen where he often sculpts his fare with gloved hands, spinning sugar or shaping dough into a three-dimensional floral confection.

Working at the Hotel Bristol where distinguished diplomats and politicians have come to expect whatever they wish for their own palate, Chef Tabourdiau responds with individual portraits of a customer's request. "At times that may mean using ingredients that are out of season," notes the chef. But in addition to the fixed menu, he cooks to order and to please.

At the hotel since 1980, the chef's cooking has been described as "cuisine that evolves." In other words, he takes classic foundations and modernizes them, trying new ingredients (especially Asian ones, because he visits the Far East each year), which eventually lead to a whole new dish. "My cooking involves a lot of mixing of flavors, steaming and roasting, and not as much emphasis on sauces," he explains. The Shrimp Salad with Candied Ginger is a good example of his approach to the lighter side. Instead of a heavy stuffing, he fills the salad with vegetables.

Hotel Le Bristol is seventy years old and embodies its own artistic expression in the noble oval hall with oak paneling and tapestry. Chef Tabourdiau says he cannot paint. Yet he can — perhaps not with a brush on a real canvas, but there is no disputing his Impressionist leanings in the plates that leave his kitchen. ❖

## Wine Suggestion

**Ruffino Orvieto Classico.** The crisp, dry, almond-scented Orvieto is perfect with seafood and maintains its balance and character even when ginger is called for in a recipe. One of Italy's best examples of a Gothic cathedral sits within the village of Orvieto.

# Shrimp Salad with Candied Ginger

*An Oriental influence punctuates this splendid salad with delicate flavor.*

2   (2-inch) pieces ginger root

⅓   cup sugar

2   cups water

24  langoustines or prawns, head on or substitute large shrimp or meat from 1 large pre-cooked lobster, cut into pieces

2   zucchini (1 pound)

4   medium tomatoes

1   shallot, peeled and finely chopped

1   garlic clove, peeled and minced

   Salt and freshly ground pepper

3   tablespoons vinegar

1   cup olive oil

¼   cup chopped cilantro

1   head green leaf lettuce

Peel the ginger and cut it into a thin julienne. Place the ginger in a small saucepan with the sugar and the water. Bring to a boil over medium heat. Reduce the heat and simmer for about 20 minutes or until the ginger is candied.

While the ginger is cooking, peel the langoustines and remove the heads. Devein them by cutting through the back and removing the dark intestinal vein.

Trim the ends of the zucchini and remove thin strips of zucchini skin at regular intervals to create a decorative pattern on the skin. Slice the zucchini thinly.

Stem 3 of the tomatoes and score the bases with an X. (This allows easier peeling after it is parboiled.) Bring a medium saucepan of water to a boil and plunge the tomatoes in for about 10 to 20 seconds or until the peel on the base starts to separate. Transfer the tomatoes to a cold water bath to stop the cooking. When the tomatoes are cool enough to handle, cut them in half, squeeze out the seeds and cut them into thin slices.

Combine the shallot and garlic in a small bowl and season to taste with salt and pepper. Whisk in 3 tablespoons vinegar and ½ cup of the oil. Add the cilantro.

Remove about 2 teaspoons of the candied ginger from the saucepan and cut it into a small dice. Stir it into the vinaigrette.

Season the langoustines or prawns with salt and pepper to taste. Pour 2 tablespoons of oil into each of 3 medium sauté pans. Heat the oil, and add the shrimp to 1 pan, the zucchini slices to another, and the tomato slices to a third. Sauté the shrimp for 2 minutes on 1 side. Meanwhile, sauté the zucchini and tomatoes very briefly, turning them after about 10 seconds. Transfer the tomatoes to the pan with the zucchini, stacking them on top. Remove the pan from the heat and set aside. Turn the shrimp and sauté them on the other side for 2 more minutes or until they are opaque but still moist.

Put the shrimp into a bowl with about $1/3$ of the vinaigrette. Toss to combine. Add the lettuce with 2 tablespoons of the remaining vinaigrette.

To serve, arrange 4 to 6 slices of tomatoes around the edge of a dinner plate. Arrange the zucchini slices around an inner circle. Twist some of the lettuce into a bouquet and place it in the center of the plate. Toss the shrimp again before arranging them on top of the tomatoes. Spoon the remaining vinaigrette over the salad and garnish with a few strips of candied ginger. Yield: 4 servings. ❖

*Cooking vegetables and fruits with sugar and water is called "candying."*

S I M I

*Sauvignon Blanc*

SONOMA COUNTY

## Wine Suggestion

**Simi Sauvignon Blanc.** Fresh oysters and other shellfish beg for a wine that is equally fresh, bracing, and somewhat smokey. Sommeliers recommend a sauvignon blanc with this dish and then proceed to drink to your good health.

# Fricassée of Oysters with Baby Vegetables

*Snow peas, radishes, and turnips lead a parade around the oysters.*
*You will need parchment paper to prepare this dish.*

2   dozen oysters, (preferably Belon)

12   baby radishes, washed and greens trimmed, tip end removed, only if necessary

12   baby carrots, greens trimmed

12   baby turnips with greens, or 2 or 3 small turnips cut into quarters

1³/₄   sticks butter

    Salt

12   large green onions, greens trimmed to 2 inches

¹/₂   cup snow peas, veins removed

12   cherry tomatoes

¹/₂   cup Beaumes de Venise or other dessert wine such as Muscat Cannelli

¹/₄   cup minced chives

Place an oyster, curved-side down on a work surface. Insert a paring knife into the hinged end of the oyster and turn the knife until the shell releases and opens. Scrape through the muscle under the oyster to release it from the shell. Scrape the oyster into a bowl and discard the shells. Continue until you have opened all the oysters. Set aside.

In a medium saucepan, place the radishes, carrots, and turnips. Add enough water to cover. Add 3 tablespoons of the butter, and salt to taste. Place a disk of parchment paper, cut to the same size as the saucepan, on top of the vegetables and simmer them for 3 to 4 minutes or until they are tender but not soft. (The disk of parchment paper prevents the liquid from evaporating and promotes a more even cooking of the vegetables). In another saucepan, add the green onions and snow peas. Add enough water to cover. In another saucepan, add enough water to cover. Add 2 tablespoons of butter. Salt to taste. Cover with a disk of parchment paper and simmer for 2 to 3 minutes or until they are tender but not too soft. Shake the pans once in a while to stir the vegetables while they are cooking.

Remove the radishes from the pan and cut them into 3 or 4 slices lengthwise, leaving the top end still attached so the radishes can be decoratively fanned. Set aside. Transfer the radishes and the other vegetables into one saucepan. Replace the disk of parchment paper. Set aside, and keep warm.

In another saucepan, simmer over medium heat for two minutes (or until they start to soften), the cherry tomatoes, ¼ cup of water, and 1 tablespoon of butter. Transfer to the saucepan with the other vegetables.

Strain the oysters through a fine mesh strainer, reserving the liquid. Heat 2 tablespoons of butter in a large sauté pan over medium heat and sauté the oysters for 1 to 2 minutes, stirring them until they are just warm. Remove the paper disk from the vegetables and add the oysters. Replace the paper, set the saucepan aside and keep warm.

Add the reserved oyster liquid to the saucepan where you have sautéed the oysters and bring to a boil. Add the wine and reduce the liquid by ¼ over high heat. Gradually whisk in 6 tablespoons butter to the reduced liquid. (Check the consistency of the sauce by dribbling it from your spoon. It should be thin with a shiny, velvety texture.) Strain the sauce onto the combination of vegetables and oysters, and stir to combine. Add 2 tablespoons of the chives.

To serve, arrange 3 radishes on each plate, spreading them out in a fan shape. Pile the oyster and vegetable fricassée in the center of the plate and spoon some sauce overtop. Garnish with the remaining chives. Yield: 4 servings. ❖

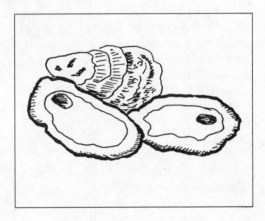

# A Medal-Winner of Olympic Status
## *Chef Guy Legay*
### HOTEL RITZ, PARIS

Guy Legay is undeniably a celebrated European chef recognized for his skill in the kitchen, and for his role in education. The Ritz-Escoffier school resides at the hotel, and when students complete their work, they join the elite of the cooking world.

Chef Legay certainly has received recognition of Olympic proportions, having clenched gold medals and similar awards from Prosper Montagne, Tattinger, the French Culinary Academy, and the Society of Paris Cooks.

The Ritz has many exquisite restaurants and Guy is in charge of them all, constantly adding new dishes and changing the menus. "I believe that it is necessary to try new ideas. A dish which is very appreciated today, could very easily be of no interest tomorrow," he says.

The chef reveals that his secret to success is, "surrounding myself with talented assistants, and of course, knowing how to pick them in the first place." (Just such an important extension of Chef Legay's food service at The Ritz is the sommelier, who says he tastes some five to six thousand different wines a year, and is often called upon to serve the oldest drink available at the hotel: an 1812 cognac.)

There is no doubt that this hotel is the perfect environment for a renowned chef. Auguste Escoffier, for whom the school is named, had advanced the prestige of French cookery. As one head of state described him, "I am the emperor of Germany but you are the emperor of chefs." Escoffier created numerous recipes that have become legendary such as peach Melba, named in honor of Austrian singer Nellie Melba. The culinary writings of Escoffier are texts of authority and part of the school's library.

It is fitting that Chef Guy Legay should work in the shadow of such a revered figure in his field. His philosophies of innovation are similar; just take a look at the baked apple recipe. You have to wonder if he isn't another Escoffier in his own right. ❖

# Almond-Butter-Stuffed Baked Apples with Pistachios

*Such a well-known favorite is given a superb new twist with
vanilla beans, almonds, and pistachios.*

5  *large tart apples*

5  *tablespoons butter, softened*

1  *cup sugar*

³⁄₄  *cup ground almonds*

1  *egg*

¹⁄₄  *cup rum*

¹⁄₂  *cup water*

1  *vanilla bean*

1  *pint pistachio ice cream,
   softened*

¹⁄₄  *cup pistachios for garnish*

Trim off the bottom and top of the apples and core them. Scoop out the flesh of 4 of the apples using a paring knife, being sure to leave the skin intact. Peel the remaining apple.

In a medium mixing bowl, blend with a fork 3 tablespoons of the butter, ²⁄₃ cup of the sugar, the almonds and egg. Blend the mixture with a fork until a uniform paste forms. Add 2 tablespoons of the rum and blend well. Preheat the oven to 325°.

Fill 4 of the apples with this mixture, covering the peeled top of the apples with some of the filling. Place the apples in a baking dish, rubbing them with the remaining butter. Add the remaining apple to the dish and sprinkle it with the rest of the sugar. Split the vanilla bean in half lengthwise and add it to the dish. Pour the water into the base of the baking dish.

Bake the apples for 1¹⁄₂ hours or until they are just tender. Remove the apples from the oven. Purée the peeled apple in a blender or food processor. Put it in a small bowl, strain the accumulated cooking juices over it and add the remaining rum. Stir to blend.

Spoon some of the apple purée in the center of a large dinner plate and place a baked apple on top. Cut off ¹⁄₄ inch of the vanilla bean and use it as a stem, to garnish the apple. Add a scoop of pistachio ice cream to the plate, swirling it together with the apple purée. Chop the pistachios and sprinkle them over the plates. Yield: 4 servings. ❖

## Win
## Sugges

**Moët & Cha
Brut Impéri**
This enticing
perfect as a
ideal for bru
Brut non-vin
champagne v
soft creamy
and complex
offers versat
can be serve
throughout a
with virtually
type of food.
extra special
the baked ap
a glass of ch
in place of a
afternoon te

# Leaving a Trail of Satisfied Palates at Home and Abroad
## *Chef Jean-Louis Taillebaud*
### ECOLE DE GASTRONOMIE FRANÇAISE, HOTEL RITZ, PARIS

The bourgeoisie family members for whom Madame Louise Bavouzet cooked, were the pleased recipients of a skilled hand. But they were not the only beneficiaries of the fine cuisinière's creations. One day, Bavouzet's crafting at the stove would prove to have even more reaching effects. Tugging curiously at her side was her grandson, who would soon echo her passion for cooking.

This budding young offspring is none other than Jean-Louis Taillebaud, who now has the inexperienced and eager, as well as the classically trained and experienced, taking note of every move he makes in the kitchen. As chef de cuisine at the Ritz since 1992, he often teaches classical cooking with a hint of the contemporary to students in his kitchen.

Before he arrived at the famous Ritz and its renowned gastronomic school of Escoffier, he decided to travel some. Chef Taillebaud, who began his career as an apprentice at fifteen years old, worked eight years as a chef in some of the best family restaurants in France's Berry region. But then the highly motivated Jean-Louis wanted to learn another language and experience other lands.

He obtained a position in London at Le Poulbot. Over the next several years, he helped build and expand the Albert and Michel Roux empire of London restaurants. By 1979, he had opened his own restaurant, Interlude de Tabaillau. He sold it in 1986 and went to Philadelphia, again expanding his horizons – this time by consulting for Trust House Forte's Palace Hotel.

In 1988, Jean-Louis moved to Ireland as executive chef at Dublin's Whites on the Green (then Ireland's most lauded restaurant). He opened another restaurant, La Vie en Rose, to rave reviews and an unprecedented guest waiting list. Chef Taillebaud has come a long way from his grandmother's side to be tableside with his own distinguished guests, now in awe of *his* talents. ❖

# Chocolate Terrine with Mocha-Vanilla Sauce

*A mousse-like dessert, this recipe is easy to do and can be made ahead.*

## Terrine:

5 ¼  ounces bittersweet
      chocolate

 ¾  ounces bitter chocolate

 3  tablespoons unsweetened
    cocoa powder

 3  tablespoons butter

 5  egg yolks

10  tablespoons confectioners'
    sugar

10  egg whites

⅛  teaspoon salt

 6  tablespoons heavy cream

## Custard:

½  cup heavy cream

 2  cups milk

 1  vanilla bean

 5  egg yolks

¾  cup sugar

 1  tablespoon powdered
    instant coffee

Line a 3 x 6 ½-inch bread-baking or terrine pan with parchment paper. In a medium bowl, combine the 2 kinds of chocolate. Add the cocoa powder and butter. Cover the bowl with aluminum foil. Set aside. Bring a medium saucepan of water to a bowl and remove it from the heat. Make a double boiler by placing the bowl with the chocolate on top of the saucepan and stirring until the chocolate melts.

In another bowl, whisk in the egg yolks and 6 tablespoons of the confectioners' sugar. Continue whisking until well blended. Set aside.

In a bowl of electric mixer, whip the egg whites and salt at medium speed until light but not dry. While the egg whites are whipping, pour the cream into a medium bowl. Whisk until light and fluffy. Set aside. Increase the speed on the mixer and add the remaining confectioners' sugar to the egg whites. Beat until the whites are quite stiff.

Stir the chocolate-butter mixture into the egg-yolk-confectioners'-sugar-mixture, blending well. Fold half of the egg whites into the chocolate mixture to lighten it. Fold in the remaining egg whites, working quickly to avoid deflating the mixture too much. Fold in the whipped cream.

Pour the mixture into the prepared mold. Cover with plastic wrap and refrigerate until the chocolate sets up or molds, at least 6 hours but preferably overnight.

*(continued)*

# Wine Suggestion

**Moët & Chandon Black Star Demi-Sec.** A slightly sweet champagne to end a great meal.

Make the custard. Combine the $1/2$ cup of cream and milk in a saucepan. Add the vanilla bean and bring the mixture to a boil. Put the egg yolks into a medium bowl, add the sugar, and whisk until the mixture is smooth and lemon-colored. Whisk in the coffee and set aside.

Pour the hot custard into the egg yolk-sugar-and-coffee mixture, whisking constantly to prevent the eggs from overcooking. Return the mixture to the saucepan and cook over medium heat, stirring constantly, until it thickens. Check the consistency by running your finger down the back of the wooden spoon you are stirring with. When the custard is thick enough, the trace of the edge you make with your finger will remain. Strain the sauce through a mesh strainer, using a wooden spoon or spatula to help push the cream through the mesh. Set aside.

Remove the chocolate terrine from the refrigerator and unmold it by running a knife between the paper and the sides of the mold. Invert the mold onto a flat surface. Remove the paper. Dip the blade of a thin knife into hot water and slice the terrine. Cover the center of an individual dessert plate with 2 to 3 tablespoons of the sauce. Place 2 slices of the chocolate terrine on top. Yield: 8 servings. ❖

*When opening champagne, keep your thumb on top of the cork until the bottle has been opened. Tilt the bottle slightly, remove the foil and wire cage (keep that thumb on the cork), then grasp the cork securely and turn the bottle, not the cork itself, to open. During this procedure, tilt the bottle away from people and windows. As the cork rises out of the bottle you will begin to feel the release of a considerable amount of pressure. While turning the bottle to remove the cork, push the cork down to assure a gentle "kiss" rather than a full blown pop.*

# In This Region, Champagne Is the Product of the Area
## *Chef Bernard Dance*
### CHÂTEAU DE SARAN, EPERNAY

At first sight, Bernard Dance appears to be as lively as his name. He may not tap his feet or perform a pas de deux while cooking, but his effervescent personality and youth would certainly permit him to do so.

In France, Bernard Dance is known for the sparkling cuisine that he offers guests of the Château de Saran. His interest in fine food can be traced to his childhood and the importance that his parents placed on spending time at the dinner table as a family. Growing up near Lyon, one of the great gastronomic regions of France, helped to create the sense of joy that Bernard feels whenever he is in the kitchen. "In order to be a good cook, you have to enjoy food," muses Chef Dance. He credits this love of food, and being so close to Lyon, for launching his career.

But, in addition to the food, Chef Dance found himself working in wine producing

regions, such as Beaujolais. "The two most important things in food are working with good natural products and good wine," says Bernard. For that reason, he began to explore the Champagne region and became quite enthusiastic about working with champagne in his recipes.

He is known for delicately balancing the champagne in his cooking so that it enhances flavor – as in the chicken dish he shares with us here – and is never overpowering. "Food has power," says Dance. Chef Dance is interested in using fresh regional products wherever possible. In Epernay, that means champagne.

Bernard Dance became head chef at Moët & Chandon's Château de Saran in 1984. During the winter months, he organizes gourmet weekends throughout the world and is quickly gaining a reputation as one of France's great chefs. ❖

*"There's no good cuisine without wine and there's no good wine without cuisine."*

*– Dance*

# Lobster Imperial

*Serve this light and elegant dish for an appetizer or as part of a special brunch.*
*This version includes champagne for a sparkling rendition.*

## Wine Suggestion

**Cuvée Dom Pérignon Rosé.**
The enticing pale rose color lends a regal air to this prestige cuvée from Moët & Chandon.

1   carrot, peeled, coarsely chopped

4   parsley stems

2   medium onions, peeled

3   bay leaves

1   sprig fresh thyme

$^{1}/_{2}$   branch celery, cut into 1-inch pieces

    Salt and freshly ground pepper

4   (1$^{1}/_{4}$ pound) live lobsters

16   green beans, strings removed (haricot verts)

### Sauce:

4   tablespoons mayonnaise

4   tablespoons heavy cream

$^{1}/_{8}$   teaspoon lemon pepper

1   tablespoon chopped parsley

1   tablespoon dry champagne or 2 teaspoons lemon or lime zest

1   medium avocado, peeled and seeded, and cut into triangles for garnish

8   chive stems for garnish

Place the carrots into a large stockpot of boiling water, filled $^{3}/_{4}$ of the way full. Add the parsley stems, onions, bay leaves, thyme and the celery. Season with salt and pepper. Add the lobsters, making sure that they are completely immersed in the water. (This will ensure that they cook evenly throughout.)

While the lobsters are cooking, fill a medium saucepan with salted water and bring it to a boil on high heat. Once the water has come to a boil, the beans can be added to cook for 3 minutes, or until tender, but still crisp. When the haricot verts are cooked, remove them from the heat, strain them in a colander and plunge them into an ice bath to stop the cooking process.

After the lobsters have begun to turn bright red, about 10 minutes, remove them from the stove and place them on a plate using a slotted spoon. (It is important to remove the lobsters from the boiling water once they have turned red because if they continue to cook, the meat will become tough.)

Set the lobster aside, and remove the beans from the ice bath. Place them on a serving plate. Place the lobsters on a cutting board and separate the claws from the body with either a sharp chef's knife or your hands. Remove the tails, cut them down the center vertically and remove the tail meat. Remove the meat from the claws, being careful to leave the meat intact for the plate presentation. Place the tail meat on the cutting board and slice the tail horizontally into 5 equal portions, ⅛-inch thick.

On individual serving plates, place the sliced tail meat down the center of the plate with the claw meat to both the left and right sides at the top, so that the pieces begin to resemble a whole lobster. Set the plates in the refrigerator to chill while making the sauce.

In a medium bowl, add the mayonnaise and the heavy cream and whisk to combine well. Season with the lemon pepper and salt. Add the chopped parsley and blend the mixture until it is a smooth paste. Whisk in the champagne and set the bowl aside.

Remove the plates with the lobster from the refrigerator and where the head should be, arrange the avocado triangles to form a stylized head. Trim the beans to equal lengths of 1 inch, and place 4 around each side of the tail.

Spoon 2 tablespoons of the sauce over the claw meat and along where the neck would be. Insert 2 chives for antennae and serve. Yield: 4 servings.  ❖

## Wine Suggestion

**Moët & Chandon White Star.** A crisp and lively champagne with character will complement any chicken dish, from a simple sauté to a richer preparation that includes a cream sauce.

# Champagne Chicken with Caramelized Onions and Chanterelle Mushrooms

*This hearty chicken dish is given a more refined flavor by the addition of champagne vinegar and chanterelle mushrooms.*

2 whole chickens, 2 pounds each
2 tablespoons vegetable oil
7 tablespoons butter
   Salt and freshly ground pepper
3 large button mushrooms, stems removed and saved for another recipe
1/2 branch celery, cut into 1/4-inch dice
1/2 medium onion, coarsely chopped
2 whole bay leaves
3 sprigs fresh thyme
8 pearl onions, peeled and sliced in half
1 tablespoon sugar
1/2 cup water
1 pound chanterelle mushrooms, stems removed and saved for another recipe
4 ounces bacon, diced into 1/4-inch cubes
1 pound potatoes, peeled and cut finely into 1/8-inch dice
1/2 cup champagne vinegar, or white wine vinegar
2 cups beef stock
3 sprigs fresh thyme for garnish

Remove the legs and thighs from both chickens and then separate the legs from the thighs by cutting through the connecting joints. Remove the breast meat from both chickens by slicing along the rib cage and wishbones. Remove the wings from the breasts at the joint and set aside. Cut the flesh of the legs away from the bone at the knee joints, scraping down the entire length of the leg bones. Pull the flesh and skin away from the bone of the legs removing the leg bones entirely. Do the same for the thighs and remove the thigh bones. Separate the wing tip from the wing and set the chicken pieces aside.

Preheat the oven to 350°. Place a medium oven-proof skillet on the stove on medium heat and add the oil along with 2 tablespoons of the butter. Season the chicken pieces on both sides with salt and pepper and add the chicken to the saucepan with the oil and butter. Sauté the chicken on both sides until the skin turns golden brown and the skin is tender, about 5 minutes. Add the button mushrooms, celery, onions, bay leaves, and 3 sprigs of thyme to the skillet. Sauté for 3 minutes, stirring constantly. Place the skillet into the oven for 20 minutes. While the chicken is baking, prepare the remaining ingredients.

In a small saucepan on medium-high heat, add the pearl onions and 2 tablespoons of the butter. Sauté for 2 minutes. Add the sugar and water and cook until the onions start to caramelize, stirring the onions constantly. Once the onions begin caramelizing, lower the heat to cook the onions slowly.

Meanwhile, slice the chanterelle mushrooms in half and set aside. In a small skillet on high flame, sauté 1 tablespoon of the butter with the chanterelles. Season with salt and pepper and continue to sauté, stirring constantly. Add the bacon, 1 tablespoon of the butter, and the diced potatoes. Cook for 5 minutes. Stir the ingredients often and cook until the potatoes are tender. Remove the skillet from the stove and set aside.

Stir the pearl onions to prevent burning, and check to see if the chicken is ready. When the flesh is firm and the juices run clear, remove the chicken from the oven and drain all of the liquid from the skillet into a stainless steel bowl. Put the skillet with the chicken back on the stove on medium heat and add the vinegar. Shake the skillet to loosen any cooked particles. Add the beef stock, bring to a boil and then lower the heat to a simmer for 10 minutes, or until the stock is reduced by $1/3$. Remove the chicken from the skillet and set it on a platter. Strain the sauce through a strainer or sieve into a small saucepan. Whisk in the last tablespoon of the butter. Taste for flavor and season if necessary. Place 2 pieces of chicken on each plate, and arrange the mushrooms and potatoes around the sides. Spoon some of the sauce across the meat and garnish with fresh thyme. Yield: 6 servings. ❖

# A Globe-Trotting Ambassador of French Cuisine
## *Chef Joseph Thuet*
LE TRIANON, EPERNAY

Chef Joseph Thuet never tires of traveling the world over to teach others the fine art of French cooking. This dedication to teaching young aspiring chefs stems from his childhood, during which time he was mentored by his uncle, a very generous man who gave Joseph much more than money could ever buy. "I chose my profession and it was inspired by my uncle, who was a great chef," he explains. "I went to his restaurant often and helped around the kitchen, cutting vegetables." After several years of general kitchen work, Joseph was trained by his uncle in the art of pastry-making, and then enrolled in a school in Paris for more formal culinary training.

Joseph Thuet began his career as a chef at L'Auberge Pontchartrain where he stayed for two years until moving to the Hotel Plaza Athenée in Paris. After serving in the military, he went to Switzerland where he gained more experience by cooking in some of the most renowned restaurants of that country. Finally, he went to Champagne where he took a position with Moët & Chandon as head Chef of Le Trianon restaurant when it opened some 26 years ago.

He describes the food of his region as "meticulous cuisine" and enjoys cooking up many sauces with champagne, such as the one for the veal and mushroom dish here.

Chef Thuet is the recipient of many culinary titles, among them the Maître Cuisinier de France and the Gold Medal Comité National de Gastronomie. He conducts and participates in gastronomic events world-wide, because it gives him the opportunity to teach others about French cooking the way he was once taught by his uncle. ❖

# Veal Medallions with Chanterelle Mushrooms and Champagne

*When buying the veal for this recipe try to find range-fed veal, as its flavor is superior.*

2 pounds veal tenderloin, sliced into 8 (4-ounce) filets

½ cup olive oil

12 ounces chanterelle mushrooms, sliced thinly

Salt and freshly ground pepper to taste

4 large button mushrooms, sliced thinly

3 shallots, peeled

2 bay leaves

3 sprigs fresh thyme

1 medium tomato, sliced in half and coarsely chopped

1 cup brut champagne

3 cups reduced beef stock

1 cup all-purpose flour

1 tablespoon butter

1 bunch fresh chives, chopped finely

Trim the fat and silver skin from the veal loin and slice the loin into 4 (8-ounce) portions, about 1-inch thick. Set aside.

Place a large skillet on the stove on high heat and add 3 tablespoons of the olive oil. Place the chanterelles into the skillet and sauté until tender, about 5 minutes. Season with salt and pepper. Add 2 more tablespoons of oil to the skillet and add the button mushrooms and shallots. Sauté until the mushrooms are browned, about 5 minutes. Add the bay leaves, thyme, and tomato. Stir the mushrooms well and season if necessary. Pour in ¼ cup of the champagne, the reduced beef stock, and stir well to combine the ingredients.

In separate skillet on high heat, add 2 tablespoons of the olive oil, rub the medallions with salt and pepper and dip them in flour. Shake off any excess flour or a thick batter will form that can burn. Add the veal to the skillet and sauté quickly on each side for about 3 minutes. While the veal is cooking, add 1 tablespoon of butter to the sauce with the mushrooms, along with the remaining champagne, and season to taste. Lower the heat on the veal and keep warm. Place ½ of the chopped chives into the sauce with the mushrooms and use the other half to garnish the veal medallions. Place 2 medallions on each serving plate, spoon the mushroom sauce across the top and sprinkle with the remaining chopped chives. Yield: 4 servings. ❖

# Wine Suggestion

**Moët & Chandon Brut Impérial Vintage.** The indication of a vintage on a champagne label means that grapes from that year's harvest were used to make the wine. Veal and mushrooms provide interesting textures and flavor which the champagne will only enhance. Brut Impérial is named for Napoleon I, who visited the cellars of Moët & Chandon and enjoyed its champagne.

# Raisin Soufflé

*Serve this wonderful, easy-to-make, and airy dessert to impress your friends.
The recipe includes the making of a pastry cream.*

2    *cups milk*

1    *vanilla bean*

2    *cups golden raisins*

1/4  *cup plus 1 tablespoon
     champagne*

3    *tablespoons all-
     purpose flour*

3    *egg yolks*

7    *tablespoons sugar*

1/8  *teaspoon salt*

4    *tablespoons butter,
     softened*

5    *egg whites*

Pour the milk into a large saucepan. Add the vanilla bean, and bring to a boil. While the milk is heating, place the raisins and 1/4 cup of champagne together in a small saucepan over medium heat. This will soften the raisins and infuse the flavor of the champagne.

In a mixing bowl, combine the flour, yolks, 3 tablespoons of the sugar, 1 tablespoon of champagne, and the salt. Mix the ingredients well to prevent lumping. Once the milk has come to a boil, add 1/3 of it to the yolk-and-flour mixture, and whisk well. (This will make the temperature of the eggs equal to that of the milk and prevent curdling.) Once the eggs are heated, pour the mixture back into the saucepan with the remaining milk. Lower the heat and constantly stir to prevent sticking and lumping. Once the pasty cream has begun to form a thick, heavy paste, remove the saucepan from the heat and set aside.

Preheat the oven to 425°. Prepare the soufflé dishes by brushing the inside of a large soufflé dish with the butter. Coat the butter with 2 tablespoons of the sugar. Set aside.

Place the egg whites into the bowl of an electric mixer. Whip on high speed and add the remaining 2 tablespoons of sugar in 3 stages, incorporating it slowly. Once the whites have reached firm peaks, fold half of the whites into the pastry cream mixture to lighten the mix. Fold in the raisins. Fold in the other half of the whites to prevent collapsing the whites. Pour this mixture into the soufflé dish. Bake in the oven for about 25 minutes, or until the top has puffed and the outside of the meringue has turned golden brown. This dish must be served immediately. Yield: 4 servings. ❖

# Sunsets as Pink as the Champagne
## *Chef Christophe Blot*
### LE ROYAL CHAMPAGNE, CHAMPILLON

From its commanding location on the Mountain of Rheims, surrounded by miles of vineyards in the Champagne region, the Royal Champagne looks out across the River Marne to the more distant vineyards of the Côte des Blancs and west to the historic Abbey of Hautvillers, where Dom Pérignon was cellar master.

Years ago, French and foreign regiments stopped by the inn during their journeys, popping the corks of countless bottles of champagne in the traditional military manner – with a saber.

Today, the Relais & Chateau inn has a Napoleonic theme that pays tribute to its past and salutes its present – colorful flower boxes filled with geraniums, and high-quality cuisine offered up by a prized chef.

Chef Christophe Blot has a commanding role at the inn, directing his staff to march out cordially and elegantly with the best the region has to offer, from fresh-caught fish to vintage wines.

The bounty of fresh ingredients found in the region of Champagne, provides Chef Blot with a great deal of latitude in preparing his cuisine. And because he likes to "see the countryside," he can often be found roaming the fields and wading through cold rivers, literally "fishing around" for the freshest products available. Inevitably, this quest leads him to one of the most prized ingredients of all, the one that takes its name from the region, the wine known simply as *champagne*. When he returns to his kitchen, the Chef can be seen gently mixing up a combination of ingredients which most often includes this rich and lively wine that adds a sparkle to everything it touches.

It is indeed the countryside itself that is responsible for the fine products that Chef Blot uses. And what a countryside it is – rolling hills and acres of vineyards where the sunsets are the color of rosé Champagne. ❖

# Filet of Beef Tenderloin au Vin Rouge

*This dish makes for an easy yet elegant main course for a special evening at home or for company.*

## Wine Suggestion

**Moët & Chandon Brut Impérial Rosé.** The complex flavors and excellent structure imparted to this champagne from the red Pinot Noir grape, makes it a fine choice with a variety of beef dishes. Brut Impérial is a great way to begin a meal as well.

3   tablespoons butter

3   pounds beef bones and scrap meat

4   cups red wine

2   carrots, peeled and coarsely chopped

1   medium tomato, cored and coarsely chopped

5   shallots, peeled, and coarsely chopped

4   tablespoons olive oil

1   pound baking potatoes, peeled and thinly sliced

    Salt and freshly ground pepper

3   cups beef stock

2   pounds beef tenderloin, cut into 8-ounce filets

$\frac{1}{2}$   cup coarsely chopped Italian parsley

Place a stockpot on the stove on medium heat and add 1 tablespoon of the butter to melt. Add the scraps and bones and sauté until the bones begin to turn golden and the scraps cook through. Add 3 cups of the red wine to the stockpot with the carrots, tomato, and half of the shallots, and bring to a slow simmer. Cook until reduced by $\frac{1}{3}$.

In a medium skillet over medium flame, heat 1 tablespoon of the olive oil. Add the potatoes. Season with salt and pepper and stir constantly to prevent sticking and burning. Sauté the potatoes until they are golden brown and tender, about 20 minutes.

Once the vegetables and wine have reduced, remove them from the stove, strain and pour the liquid into a saucepan. Add the beef stock and the rest of the wine and reduce by $\frac{1}{3}$. Remove the potatoes from the stove and keep warm.

In a large skillet, add the remaining olive oil and the beef filets, and sauté over high heat on both sides to brown the meat. Once the meat has browned, add the remaining shallots and 1 tablespoon of the butter. Sauté until the shallots are tender and remove the beef from the skillet, keeping warm for later. Deglaze the pan with 1 cup of the reducing stock. Simmer for 3 minutes, strain and add the strained liquid back into the reducing stock. Finish the sauce by whisking in the remaining butter. Set aside.

Place 1 filet on each serving plate, with the potatoes and 1 teaspoon of the diced shallots. Pour sauce across the filets and garnish with Italian parsley. Yield: 4 servings. ❖

# Capon with Smoked Ham and Red Wine Sauce

*The game flavor of the capon, with the addition of the cured pork and red wine,*
*offers an evocative dish of smoky tastes.*

## Wine Suggestion

**Moët & Chandon Brut Impérial Vintage.** This elegant and refined champagne can be enjoyed throughout the meal and will surely capture the attention of even the most discriminating gourmet.

4½ tablespoons butter

1 ripe medium tomato, diced into ½ inch cubes

1 carrot, cut into ⅛-inch thick slices

1 rib celery, coarsely chopped

2 shallots, coarsely chopped

4 sprigs Italian parsley

1 capon (3 pounds)

2 cups red wine

5 tablespoons olive oil

Salt and freshly ground pepper

12 pearl onions, peeled

½ pound bacon, julienned into ⅛-inch slices

4 cups beef stock

2 leeks, white part only, julienned into ⅛-inch slices

¼ pound smoked ham, diced into ⅛-inch cubes

8 button mushrooms, quartered

8 sprigs Italian parsley for garnish

Heat 1 tablespoon of the butter in a large saucepan on medium heat and add the tomato, carrots, celery, shallots, and the parsley. (This mixture of ingredients is called a mirepoix, a mixture of ingredients that are used to flavor stocks and sauces.) Sauté the mirepoix for 10 minutes until tender. While the mirepoix is cooking prepare the capon.

First, remove the legs with the thighs attached. Remove the breast meat from the breast bone with the wings attached. Cut the tips from the wing joints and remove some of the flesh from the joint. With a small paring knife, poke a hole through the flesh and skin of the breast. Take the bone of the wing tip and poke it through the hole to just expose the knuckle so that the breasts resemble "little hams." Remove the bones from each thigh and any excess flesh from the joint at the knee. With a paring knife poke a hole through the middle of the flesh of the thigh. Push the leg bone through this hole. The thigh should also resemble a "little ham." Tie all 4 of the "little hams" around the outside with kitchen string. This will help hold the flesh together during cooking. Refrigerate the "little hams."

Preheat the oven to 350°. Add the red wine to the cooking mirepoix and reduce by half. Add the beef stock and simmer on low heat for 3 hours to form a glacé de viande. (Glacé de viande is a gelatinous reduction of brown stock that is very intense in flavor.) Place a large oven-proof skillet on the stove on high heat. Add 3 table-

*(continued)*

spoons of olive oil and add the "little hams." Season with salt and pepper. Sauté until golden brown, about 3 minutes on each side. Place the pan in the oven and bake for 20 minutes or until the internal temperature reaches 145° on a food thermometer.

Place a medium skillet on the stove on medium-high heat. Add 1 tablespoon of butter and add the pearl onions. Season with salt and pepper and sauté for 2 minutes. Remove the pearl onions from the skillet and add them to the chicken in the oven. In the same skillet used to sauté the pearl onions, add the bacon and sauté on medium heat for 5 minutes or until the bacon is crisp. Drain the bacon of grease and return to the skillet. Add

1 ½ tablespoons of butter and sauté the bacon with the ham and mushrooms. Season with salt and pepper. Cook until the mushrooms are tender and golden brown, about 5 minutes. Strain the glacé de viande through a sieve into a medium saucepan. Add 1 tablespoon of butter and whisk to combine.

Place a medium saucepan of water on the stove on high and bring to a boil. Blanch the leeks quickly and remove to a small bowl. Season with salt and pepper. Place the leeks onto the center of individual serving plates. Next add the bacon-ham-mushroom mixture. Drizzle a small amount of the sauce over the mushrooms and the chicken. Serve immediately. Yield: 4 servings. ❖

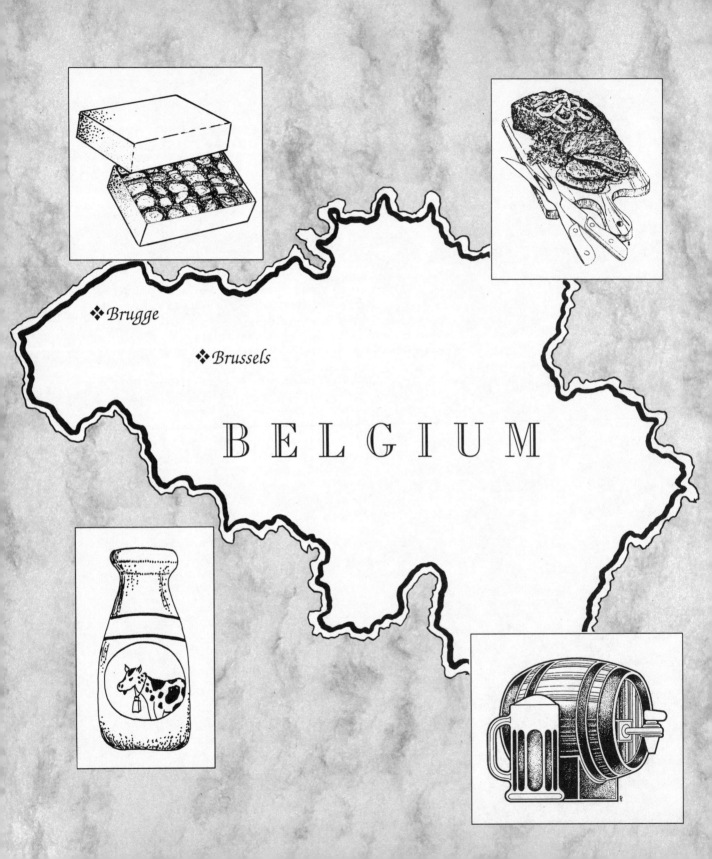

Brugge

Brussels

BELGIUM

# BELGIUM

# ... the Handwriting on the Wall: A Testament to His Talent

## *Chef Pierre Wynants*

### COMME CHEZ SOI, BRUSSELS

In 1965, he received the first prize Prosper Montagné. A decade later, he received the Golden Key Gault Millau and by 1979, three Michelin stars. Not resting on his laurel leaves, he garnered the Cook of the Year in 1988 and Grand Prize of the Kitchen Art in 1991. By 1992, not only had he clenched an award for having the most beautiful menu in Belgium, but he was named Man of the Year *(Magazine Ambiance Culinaire)* Culinary Award.

Pierre Wynants, the grandson of the founder of the restaurant he now owns, is a chef extraordinaire. Born in 1939, he began his career at sixteen as a cook at the Savoy of Brusseland and eventually went on to run the kitchen of Prince Albert, the brother of the King of England.

Tradition has played an important role at Comme Chez Soi and Chef Wynants was ready to step into the role of chef/owner successor in 1973 when his father, Louis, passed away. It was Pierre's turn to show the world how family ties have maintained the quality and integrity of Comme Chez Soi.

Chef Wynants literally opened the kitchen of the restaurant (started in 1926) to diners to watch the master behind the scenes. Some thirty guests, five nights a week, dine right in the kitchen, learning how he prepares dishes for the main dining room. Sometimes guests get up and help, and they might just be preparing the roast beef with shallot butter from the recipe presented here!

The chef's repertoire is vast and with dishes such as the Mangoes in Cognac Syrup, you can see that it is also interesting and suited to today's lifestyles. Pierre has compiled his recipes, with his latest cookbook, *L'Equilibre Gourmand,* published in 1990.

Celebrities such as Jack Nicklaus and Rod Steiger, and other luminaries actually sign their names on a wall at the restaurant. So, you can literally see the handwriting on the wall at Comme Chez Soi in more ways than one. Likely, this will always be a great place to eat. ❖

# Roast Beef with Shallot Butter Sauce

*Quick and easy, this classic favorite is made with red wine and shallots reduced,
and thickened with butter. When purchasing your filet make sure to ask the butcher for a château cut.*

## Wine Suggestion

**Simi Cabernet Sauvignon.** A richly textured and complex wine made from Cabernet Sauvignon grapes will harmonize with this Roast Beef dish, especially when the same red wine is included in the sauce.

2   shallots

$^1\!/_2$   cup red wine

$^1\!/_2$   cup demi-glace or brown sauce such as recipe on page 161

$^3\!/_4$   pound plus 3 tablespoons unsalted butter

Salt and freshly ground pepper

$^1\!/_4$   cup water

4   (8-ounce) beef filets from the loin, cleaned

Make the basis for the shallot butter sauce. Peel and finely mince the shallots and place in a heavy saucepan with the red wine. Heat over high heat and add the demi-glace, whisking to combine. Allow to reduce by one third, stirring constantly to ensure that all of the particles from the side of the pan are collected. Once the sauce is reduced (about 6 minutes), whisk in $^3\!/_4$ of a pound of the butter in 3 stages, about 3 tablespoons at a time, fully melting and incorporating. Season with salt and pepper to taste. Set aside. Preheat the oven to 375°.

Place the remaining 3 tablespoons of butter into a large sauté pan or skillet and heat until butter becomes bubbly. Place the filets into the pan and season with salt and pepper, keeping the pan tilted so that the filets are always surrounded by butter. Cook the filets for approximately 4 minutes until browned both on top and bottom, spooning butter over the top.

Place the filets in the oven and cook for an additional 10 minutes. This will produce a medium-rare filet. (For a more well-done filet, increase the cooking time.) Remove the pan from the oven. Spoon the cooking liquid over the tops of the filets and then remove them from the pan. Place them on a separate plate and set aside. Over medium heat, deglaze the filet pan with the water, bringing it to a boil. Pour contents into the shallot butter and mix well. Slice each filet into 4 slices and arrange in a fan at the bottom of the plate. Spoon the sauce horizontally across the meat and serve. Yield: 4 servings. ❖

# Mangoes in Cognac Syrup

*Mangoes are becoming increasingly popular in the United States and they are a good source of vitamins and citrus. This dessert is an elegant way to serve guests at home.*

½  ounce powdered gelatin

½  cup water

¼  cup sugar

2  tablespoons currant jelly

1  lemon

¼  cup candied grapefruit, or candied orange peel, diced

2  tablespoons Mandarin Napoleon Cognac or Grand Marnier

2  mangoes, peeled and the fruit cut (away from the seed) on an angle and into 6 wedges of equal size

1  cup fresh raspberries

Dissolve the gelatin and 2 tablespoons of cold water in a saucepan. In another saucepan over medium heat, start the syrup by whisking together the water and the sugar to combine the ingredients well. Add the currant jelly and the juice of the lemon, continuing to whisk. Add the dissolved gelatin to the cooking syrup. Whisk the mixture and allow it to come to a boil. Immediately remove the pan from the stove and strain it into a bowl that is resting inside another bowl filled with ice water. This will help to cool the syrup quickly. Add the candied grapefruit and cognac and stir.

Let the syrup cool and then spoon the syrup over the mangoes, making sure to cover the entire surface. Set this aside to marinate for approximately 4 hours in the refrigerator.

To serve, spoon the mangoes onto a plate and garnish with fresh raspberries. Yield: 4 servings. ❖

# Haute Cuisine on a Culinary Runway
## *Chef Hervé Raphanel*
### HOTEL CONRAD, BRUSSELS

In this famous metropolis of promenades, ornate architecture, and a city square full of artists capturing the slices of life that play out here every day, there is a chef known as one of Europe's finest – and at such a young age.

Chef Hervé Raphanel is already bearing one Michelin star for his twenty-nine years, and working on a second at La Maison d' Maitre at the Conrad. Those who have sat at his banquet and party tables would say that the recognition is for his expert service and custom-tailored dishes, served nonetheless luxuriously for a large group. Those who have dined at a romantic table for two here would argue that he deserves the respect for the way his meals complement a quieter evening of wine and roses.

Whichever way you look at it, Hervé Raphanel is lauded for his presentation – like a fine fashion designer – no matter the number of guests. This chef, who has been working professionally in his field since fourteen years of age, has something special to offer. You might say, he is a couturier of food – designing his own plates, with an appliqué of ingredients from all over the world.

Take, for example, the ordinarily peasant dish of cabbage and chicken he is teaching you how to do in this book. Chef Raphanel (even his name has a designer's ring) clothes the dish in delicate rice, ties the wrap, and steams it gently. He then dresses the bundles with a coating of sauce.

The pain perdu turned into a bread pudding is another showcase example of this chef's unique culinary collection. He has bejeweled the toasted French bread with facets of rich, vanilla custard and emerald pistachio ice cream.

Perhaps the best explanation of why this chef is so heralded is expressed in a comment he makes about his cooking philosophy: "I have great respect for the foundation of cooking, but at the same time, I seek certain design – just like with fashion. I am after a certain look which brings freshness and color to my cooking." If you change the word cooking to clothing in this quote, it could be something Christian Dior might say. ❖

RUFFINO

RISERVA DUCALE

Chianti Classico

Riserva

I.L.RUFFINO

750 mL

## Wine Suggestion

**Ruffino Riserva Ducale Gold Label Chianti Classico Riserva.** In Italy, where game dishes are frequently seen in season, a robust and complex Chianti Classico Riserva is often the wine of choice. A classic pairing with Cornish hen.

# Cornish Hen Bundles with Cabbage

*These hens are enveloped in edible rice paper.*
*Using rice paper allows for a dainty dish to set before your guests.*

8  *Napa cabbage leaves*

1  *pound new potatoes, peeled*

6  *tablespoons butter*

8  *ounces pearl onions, peeled*

¼  *pound bacon, diced*

½  *pound button mushrooms*

2  *Cornish game hens, approximately 1½ to 2 pounds each*

   *Salt and freshly ground pepper*

1  *cup brandy*

½  *cup chicken stock or veal demi-glace*

4  *pieces rice paper about 12 inches in diameter*

4  *scallions, blanched and cooled quickly in ice water*

   *Chopped chives for garnish*

Preheat the oven to 400°. Blanch the cabbage leaves just until their color is intensified. Immediately remove the cabbage from the stove and quickly cool in ice water. Gently squeeze out any excess water, then coarsely chop the leaves. Set aside.

Cut the potatoes into tourne shapes, resembling small footballs with 7 sides. (Make sure all of the potatoes are the same size so that they all cook evenly.)

Add 1 tablespoon of the butter to a medium size sauté pan or skillet and melt until bubbly. Add the potatoes and brown over medium heat, shaking the pan periodically to prevent burning and sticking. Make sure the potatoes are brown on all sides. Then place in the oven to finish cooking for about 10 minutes. Continue stirring the potatoes while they are cooking.

Add the onion and bacon to a medium-size saucepan and cook over low heat for about 10 minutes. Add the mushrooms and 3 tablespoons of the butter. Finish sautéing the onions, mushrooms, and bacon and remove when browned. Set aside. Add the cabbage to the saucepan and sauté, shaking continuously to prevent sticking and burning. Cook the cabbage for about 4 minutes or until tender and slightly browned.

Once the potatoes have been removed from the oven, add them to the skillet to cook for just 1 minute in order to coat with the bacon and onion juices. Set aside.

To prepare the game hen, remove the wings and both legs at the joints. Carefully slice down both sides of the breast bone and remove both breasts from the bone. Cut the remaining carcass into several pieces and season with salt and pepper. Place into a heated skillet with 1 tablespoon of melted butter, about 5 to 7 minutes or until browned. Remove the chicken. Turn the heat on high and deglaze the pan with the brandy. Add 4 tablespoons of the stock, bringing the liquid to a boil. Add the remaining stock and cook for about 15 minutes to develop full flavor.

Meanwhile, prepare the bundles. Dip the 4 pieces of rice paper into a bowl of tap water, gently shaking each piece back and forth until it is soft and pliable. Place 1 sheet on a flat surface and spoon 2 tablespoons of the cabbage mixture and some of the diced bacon in the center of each. Place $1/2$ of each breast and 1 thigh on top of the cabbage mixture, gather the paper around the chicken, and tie securely with a strip of scallion. Complete the same procedure for the three other bundles. Place the rice paper bundles into a nonstick skillet and bake in the oven for 5 to 10 minutes until the bundles start to turn golden.

While the bundles are baking, remove the bones from the stock and pour the broth through a sieve into a sauté pan or skillet. Add the remaining tablespoon of butter and bring to a boil to thicken. Season to taste. When cooked, remove the bundles from the oven and place 1 bundle in the center of each plate. Spoon the potatoes, mushrooms, and onions around the sides and pour some of the sauce from the thickened stock onto the tops of the vegetables. Garnish with chopped chives. Yield: 4 servings. ❖

# Wine Suggestion

**Moët & Chandon Black Star Demi-Sec.** This champagne has a wisp of sweetness, allowing it to blend perfectly with the taste and texture of the ice cream and pistachios.

# French Toast with Crème Anglaise and Pistachios

*Dessert time is easy with this delicious pain perdu.*

½  loaf day-old French bread (12 baguette slices)

3  whole eggs

1  cup half-and-half

1-2  tablespoons unsalted butter

¼  cup granulated sugar

2  cups crème anglaise (see page 165 for recipe)

1  pint pistachio ice cream

¼  pound pistachios, shelled and coarsely chopped for garnish

Cut the bread into ¾-inch slices. Remove the crust and then cut each slice in half diagonally. Set aside and mix the batter by whisking together the eggs and half-and-half until smooth.

Heat a sauté pan or skillet over high heat, adding 1 tablespoon of the butter to the pan. Heat until bubbly. Dip several of the bread slices into the batter making sure to coat both sides. Place them into the pan and generously sprinkle the tops with sugar. When the bottoms are browned, turn the bread over and sprinkle with more sugar and cook until browned. Use the remaining tablespoon of butter, if necessary, to sauté the remaining slices of bread in the same manner.

Remove the crème anglaise from the refrigerator and ladle a small amount onto the center of each plate. Place 3 slices of toast on each plate, top with pistachio ice cream and chopped pistachios for garnish. Yield: 4 servings. ❖

# A Little Detective Work Solves the Culinary Mystery

## *Chef Luc Huysentruyt*

### DE SNIPPE RESTAURANT, BRUGGE

Just ask veteran Chef Luc Huysentruyt why he decided to become a chef and he likely will offer, "I like to make people happy." What that translates into on a day-to-day basis is a great cook in constant search of high quality ingredients that help him offer guests an unparalleled experience at his restaurant/hotel.

Looking for those ingredients, for instance, often takes him to a local free-range chicken farm. Here they are so particular, that the proprietor marks each egg according to the hen and cock that produced it.

Belgium is noted for its beer, its lace-making, and popular detective Hercule Poirot of the Agatha Christie mystery novels. Perhaps Chef Huysentruyt takes his cue from the legendary detective, for he seems to have solved and satisfied the mystery of keeping people happy, indeed.

A favorite dish of Huysentruyt is a chicken fricassée, which is made with Belgian beer instead of wine, offering a heartier, country-style taste.

A chef for some thirty years, Luc serves a hybrid cuisine that is a combination of French, Italian, and Chinese. Meals offer diners very different flavors, all served up in the restaurateur's 12th-century house, where the chef and his wife share hospitality, charm, and their art collection of Flemish paintings – some three hundred years old.

Brugge is often called the Venice of the North, because of its winding and enchanting canals that host many remnants of Medieval days such as windmills and historic homes. De Snippe has become legend in this historical town where finding the best place to eat is no mystery at all. ❖

# Sea Scallop Soup

*This clear, delicate soup embraces the flavors of Asia with Chef Huysentruyt's interpretation.*

1 large onion, thinly sliced

½ cup celery, cut julienne

½ cup leeks, white part only, cut julienne

½ cup carrots, cut julienne

1 bay leaf

4 sprigs thyme

4 tablespoons butter

1 cup water

1 cup white wine

8 large sea scallops

Salt and freshly ground pepper

1 teaspoon curry powder

2 sprigs chervil, for garnish

In a large skillet, begin preparing the broth. Sauté the onion, celery, leeks, carrots, bay leaf, and thyme in 2 tablespoons of the butter. Add the water and wine and cook over high heat, bringing to a boil. While simmering the broth, cut the scallops into 3 horizontal slices and add them to the pan with the vegetables and broth. Season with salt and pepper.

Turn the scallops so they will poach evenly. After less than 1 minute in the broth, the flesh of the scallops begins to separate and they are ready. Transfer the scallops to a bowl and set aside.

Add the curry to the vegetables and broth, whisking to combine. Heat the broth until it is bubbly. Whisk in the remaining butter to combine. Place some of the vegetables in the bottom of individual rim soup bowls and top with the scallops. Ladle in some of the broth and garnish with the remaining vegetables and chervil. Yield: 4 servings. ❖

# Almond Tuile Baskets Filled with Berries and Sabayon Sauce

*Traditionally, tuiles are made by shaping the still-hot cookies around a rolling pin. Chef Huysentruyt gives this cookie a new shape by gently pushing the cookie into the bottom of a bowl to assimilate a tulip.*

## Tuile:

½ *pound unsalted butter*

5 *egg yolks*

⅔ *cup sugar*

½ *cup all-purpose flour*

¾ *cup coarsely chopped almonds*

½ *cup sliced, toasted almonds*

7 *egg whites*

## Sabayon sauce:

7 *egg yolks*

½ *cup sugar*

⅓ *cup sweet Marsala*

1½ *pints each fresh strawberries, blueberries, raspberries, and blackberries*

*Fresh mint for garnish*

Preheat the oven to 400°. Coat a large cookie sheet with nonstick spray. Melt the butter in a medium saucepan over medium-high heat. Remove from the fire and set aside to cool to room temperature.

In a medium bowl beat the egg yolks. Add the sugar, flour, and all of the almonds. Stir until combined. In a separate bowl, lightly froth the egg whites and add to the almond-and-yolk mixture. Pour the melted butter into this mixture and stir to blend.

Using a fork or spoon, ladle a small amount of batter onto the cookie sheet in a thin layer. A good size for each cookie is approximately 4 to 6 inches in diameter (for a 4-inch diameter bowl), but the choice of size depends on the size of the individual serving bowl you are using. Leave at least 2 inches between each cookie and bake 5 minutes or until golden brown.

Remove immediately from the oven and from the cookie sheet with a metal spatula. While still hot, nest each cookie into a small bowl and gently push to the bottom while shaping the sides to resemble a tulip. Remember to work quickly or the cookies will be too hard to shape. If this happens, just return the cookie sheet to the oven for a few seconds until the tuiles soften again.

*(continued)*

# Wine Suggestion

**Moët & Chandon White Star.** During the warm summer months, it is not unusual to see Parisian restaurants serving champagne mixed with fresh seasonal fruits. A champagne that has an ever-so-slight sweetness is an ideal accompaniment to the fresh berries and the almond.

While the cookies are cooling, begin to prepare the sabayon sauce. Pour the egg yolks, sugar, and Marsala into a medium stainless steel bowl and place overtop a similar size steaming pot of water. Whisk the

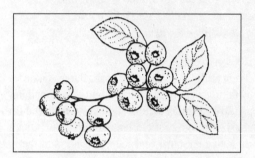

mixture quickly as the sabayon will begin to absorb air rapidly. Continue whisking for a total of approximately 4 minutes, until the sauce is very aerated and thick. (Make sure to remove the bowl from the heat if the egg mixture gets too hot, or the eggs will scramble.) Continue to whisk until slightly cooled and then return to the stove to continue the cooking process.

To serve, place one basket on each plate and fill ¾ of the way full with a combination of the berries. Spoon the sabayon sauce over the berries and serve immediately. Garnish with fresh mint if available. Yield: 6 servings. ❖

Madrid
❖

S P A I N

❖ Seville

# SPAIN

# 'Market Cuisine' Fills His Culinary Basket

## Chef Francisco Rubio Sanchez (Paco Rubio)

### GRILL NEPTUNO, MADRID

*"If when you enter the kitchen you are frustrated, the food comes out frustrated. If you are happy, the dish will note it. The frustration that comes from the house, from work, from within, or from the family should be left at the kitchen door or it will be reflected in the food."*

*– Rubio*

The blustery winds of a typical Madrid winter may have Chef Francisco Rubio Sanchez (also known as Paco Rubio) cooking up hearty soups and stews more than usual. But no matter what the season, the comestibles from this chef — one of the best known in Spain — are perennial favorites you will want to serve your own guests. One such example is the merluza on page 117 that contains the essence of Spanish cookery — a bounty of fish.

As Madrid residents leave their skyscraper jobs or tourists their shopping jaunts along the boulevards of this most cosmopolitan city, they may stop for some of Paco Rubio's cooking at the Grill Neptuno for the chef's specials.

Like many chefs, Paco Rubio searches for the freshest ingredients. Chef Rubio feels that using what is in season is its own style of cooking, and he has given it a most appropriate name: *market cuisine*. "We are looking for the best of the season to determine what we can create today," explains the chef. "Rather than using a fixed menu and trying to make it work, we go to the market and look — and from there we cook."

The chef has reliable providers who have been bringing him produce and seafood for more than a decade, and supplying the hotel for some 50 years. They have come to know what he demands.

Although his cooking is that of fundamentally Spanish cuisine, Chef Rubio is influenced by other nations as he continually travels to learn myriad styles. His cooking often takes on a French twist, for example. The chef makes a foie gras which he explains is absolutely Spanish. He makes it con escabeche or with milk (something he says the French would never do) and he includes sherry vinegar, white wine, laurel, and tomatillo.

This mixture of Spanish and French is also evident in the surroundings where the chef practices his craft. The Palace Hotel is French with an elegant Spanish atmosphere, punctuated by Renaissance paintings and a rotunda with a magnificent crystal dome under which *market cuisine* flourishes with great innovation. ❖

# Merluza with Seafood Ragoût of Shrimp and Clams

*A bountiful and festive dish features your choice of a white fish accompanied by authentic combinations of Spanish ingredients.*

4 (4-ounce) hake steaks, cod, or whiting

Salt and freshly ground pepper

All-purpose flour for dredging

¼ cup olive oil

6 medium cloves garlic, peeled and minced

12 asparagus spears, woody ends snapped

1 large onion, diced

16 cherrystone clams

20 medium shrimp, peeled and deveined

1 cup green peas

1 cup white wine

¾ cup clam broth

4 hard-cooked eggs, shells removed and eggs quartered

1 small bunch chives, finely chopped

Season the fish with salt and pepper and dredge the fish in flour to coat both sides, shaking off any excess flour. Place a large skillet on a medium-high flame. Add the olive oil and sauté the garlic. Place the fish in the skillet and sauté quickly to prevent the fish from absorbing too much oil. When the fish start to turn light golden on 1 side, turn over to cook the other side.

Meanwhile, bring 2 quarts of water to a boil in a medium saucepan. Cook the asparagus until al dente, about 3 minutes, and remove from the stove. Set aside in a warm place.

Return to the skillet and add the chopped onion and garlic, sprinkling it around the fish. Sauté for about 2 minutes swirling the pan. The onions should be translucent. Turn the fish over again and add the clams, the shrimp, peas, and white wine. Bring to a simmer and add the clam broth. Simmer for about 3 minutes and add the chives. Taste the sauce and adjust the seasoning if necessary.

When the clams have opened, keep the skillet on the stove continuing to cook the fish, but add 4 clams each and 5 shrimp around the edges of each plate. Divide the egg quarters and asparagus evenly and finally place 1 steak at the center of each plate. Pour the sauce overtop. Serve immediately. Yield: 4 servings. ❖

## Wine Suggestion

**Marqués de Riscal Rueda.** The Rueda region of Spain yields a dry white wine offering a delicate aroma and taste of violets. Perfect with all types of fish, and even spicy salsa. Marqués de Riscal is reported to be the oldest existing bodega in Rioja, founded in 1860.

# Salmon Terrine with Anchovy Butter

*Although this dish makes a splendid entrée, consider it also as a brunch item or an appetizer. The salmon makes for an unusual and surprising outer-casing for the terrine.*

## Wine Suggestion

**Simi Altaire.** The delicate, fresh-berry character of this medium-bodied red wine is an excellent foil to any salmon dish, especially one containing fresh herbs and pepper.

4  anchovy filets

6  tablespoons unsalted butter

6  tablespoons crème fraîche or sour cream

   Salt and freshly ground pepper to taste

3/4  pound smoked salmon, pounded into 1/16-inch slices (very thin)

1  head curly endive

1  head radicchio

1/4  teaspoon chopped fresh thyme

1/4  teaspoon chopped fresh savory

1/4  teaspoon chopped fresh parsley

2  tablespoons sherry vinegar

6  tablespoons olive oil

6  anchovy filets for garnish

Blend the anchovies and butter in a food processor, scraping the sides of the bowl. When a smooth paste has formed, add the crème fraîche. Season with salt and pepper to taste. Line the inside of an 8-inch loaf pan with plastic wrap with 2 inches hanging over the edge of the pan. Lay the salmon first in the bottom of the pan and then up the sides. Spoon in 1/3 of the anchovy-crème-fraîche mix and cover with a layer of salmon. Repeat until all of the anchovy mix and salmon slices are included. Cover with the overhanging sides of plastic and refrigerate overnight.

Remove the terrine from the refrigerator, unwrap the plastic cover and turn the terrine right-side up. Slice into 1/2-inch-thick slices and set aside. Wash and clean the endive and radicchio and cut into salad-size pieces. Place some of both into the center of each plate and reserve. Make a vinaigrette by mixing together the herbs, vinegar, oil, salt and pepper. Drizzle over the tops of the endive and radicchio. Place 2 terrine slices on top and garnish with anchovy filets. Yield: 6 servings. ❖

# From Flamencos to Flans and a Fancy of Fruits

## *Bernardo Santos Garcia-Muñoz*

### EL CAFÉ DE ORIENTE, MADRID

Bullfights, dusty olive trees, and flamboyant flamenco dancers, all these and more come to mind when one thinks of the character of Spain. It's a land of many provences where geography plays a key role in its variety. Spain stretches over contrasting terrains so traditions vary and the food is a mèlange of flavors and techniques. In fact, there is a saying that, "In the south, they fry. In the central regions, they roast. And in the north, they stew." Perhaps that is a an oversimplification, but one thing is certain in this great country. Food is crayon-colorful, full-bodied and robust of flavor.

And one of those they talk about, who is making noise in the culinary arena, is Chef Bernardo Santos Garcia-Muñoz.

The recipient of a Michelin star, Chef Muñoz prepares dinner at El Café de Oriente in the style of his region – Andalusia. Seafood is essential, but so is pork and vegetables.

The Andalusian region is flush with fruits because of its ideal fruit-growing climate, which also easily breeds fruits of a tropical nature. The area is also known for its brandies. The recipe here for the fruit gratin is just one example of how Chef Muñoz integrates indigenous foodstuffs into his menu. The region is mountainous, so the goat and lamb products that are produced are also typically found in the chef's kitchen.

Flans, the luscious desserts that probably most symbolize this country's sweets menu, are also a favorite at the chef's table. Again, Chef Muñoz incorporates his custards with the region's produce, using a fancy of fresh fruit in season. Such a dessert does supply a stunning closing to the chef's sumptuous dinners – delightfully Andalusian in style. ❖

119

# Hearts of Palm Salad with Tuna and Tomatoes

*Crisp vegetables and a tangy condiment offer this dish from Chef Muñoz,
a harmonious complement to the mild seafood.*

## Wine Suggestion

**Domaine Chandon Carneros Blanc de Noirs.** The strawberry tinge lends a seductive quality to this sparkling wine made according to the méthode champenoise, a method discovered by Dom Pérignon in the 17th century. The Blanc de Noirs has the character of Pinot Noir, the grape from which it is made, and is sturdy enough to handle almost any type of salad.

4   small heads bibb lettuce

2   Belgian endives

2   large ripe tomatoes, cored and quartered

8   hearts of palm

1   medium avocado, pitted and skinned

8   cooked white asparagus, (fresh preferred)

8   ounces fresh tuna broiled and well-done, cut into bite-size pieces, or canned white albacore

½   cup green Spanish olives, pitted

8   tablespoons olive oil

3   tablespoons sherry vine

Halve each head of lettuce, discarding the outer leaves. Slice in half again and use only the hearts. Reserve leaves for another recipe.

Pull apart the leaves from the endive. Core and reserve. Slice the hearts of palm and the avocado on the diagonal, and place decoratively on a serving plate with the endive, tomato and the lettuce. Top with the asparagus, tuna, and olives and spoon the oil and sherry wine overtop. Yield: 4 servings. ❖

# Gratin of Almond Cream with Pears, Peaches and Raspberries

*Spanish desserts are characterized by their use of egg-rich custards and creams accompanied by fresh fruit. This dessert is delicious and easy to make.*

1  *cup heavy cream*

2  *teaspoons pure vanilla extract*

6  *tablespoons sugar*

6  *tablespoons all-purpose flour*

4  *eggs*

1  *tablespoon blanched almonds, coarsely chopped*

2  *peaches, peeled, pitted, and cut horizontally into $\frac{1}{8}$-inch slices*

2  *Bartlett or Anjou pears, peeled, cored, and cut horizontally into $\frac{1}{8}$-inch slices*

12 *raspberries*

1  *tablespoon unsalted butter*

1  *pint vanilla ice cream*

$\frac{1}{4}$  *cup pear brandy*

In a heavy-bottomed, medium saucepan, bring the cream and vanilla to a boil over medium heat. In a separate saucepan, add the sugar and flour and whisk to combine. Add the eggs and almonds and whisk to make a smooth batter. Once the cream has come to a boil, slowly pour $\frac{1}{3}$ of the cream into the egg-and-flour mixture, whisking to make sure the ingredients are well combined and the temperature of the eggs is raised equal with the cream. Return the saucepan to the stove and lower the heat to medium-low, stirring constantly. Be sure to continually stir the almond cream to prevent burning and lumping. Cook until a thick, smooth paste is formed.

Remove the saucepan from the heat and spread the cream onto a serving plate, spreading it in a thick layer to coat the entire surface. Arrange the peach and pear slices, and the raspberries over the cream. Dot with small pieces of butter and sprinkles of sugar, and place under the broiler for 30 seconds, just to brown. Remove from the oven and scoop ice cream onto the center of the plate. Pour a small cap of brandy over-top. Serve immediately. Yield: 4 servings. ❖

# A Place Where Roasting Is an Art
## *Chef Antonio Gistau Noguera*
### HOTEL SANTA MARIA DE EL PAULAR, MADRID

Chef Antonio Noguera has worked all over Spain and Italy and has been head chef of the Hotel Santa Maria de el Paular, for the past eight years. He defines his cooking as "regional and uncomplicated."

Castellano is the style of cooking at the hotel, which means there are a lot of fish dishes prepared, and roasting is the essence of the kitchen here. Free-range meats are the order of the day, as the chef cares to serve only natural and fresh ingredients. The free-range animals he serves have been roaming without bondage on the mountains where they eat greenery and herbs.

One of the delicacies of the house is Serrano ham, which is smoked and cured and is one of the area's local specialties. A whole leg costs some five hundred dollars, but because this style ham is sliced so thinly, it goes a very long way.

The cuisine Chef Noguera serves is centered around a wood-burning brick oven where a lamb or pig may be roasted in traditional Castellano fashion. Since the fire is fueled with oak, it infuses the meat with a golden color and special taste, similar to Basque cooking.

Roasting is a hallmark of cookery in Chef Noguera's area. Expert roasters, such as this chef, know exactly when the meat will taste its best and is cooked to perfection. That is usually when the meat is no longer raw, however, it is not overly cooked either. This takes experience and especially intuition, two qualities Chef Noguera seems to have in all his dishes. ❖

# Garlic and Smoked-Pork Soup with Croustades

*The Basque love to combine savory and smoky flavors creating thick broths out
of bread and eggs, including whatever ingredients are on hand.
The culinary history of the Basque region was influenced heavily by the ancient Romans.*

2    tablespoons olive oil

5    medium cloves garlic,
     thinly sliced

¼   pound Serrano or
     Prosciutto ham, diced into
     ¼-inch cubes

1    small chorizo sausage
     (about 3 ounces), skin
     removed and diced into
     ¼-inch cubes

1    loaf french bread, sliced
     into ½ to 1-inch thick slices

1    teaspoon paprika

6    cups chicken broth

4    eggs

Heat 2 tablespoons olive oil in a 2-quart saucepan, over medium-high heat. Add the garlic, ham, and chorizo. Sauté until the meat starts to turn golden brown, about 7 minutes. Remove the saucepan from the heat and set aside.

Dip 1 side of each slice of bread into the cooking juices from the ham and chorizo. Place in a non-stick skillet, sprinkle with paprika, and sauté until crisp. Set aside and keep warm.

Place the pan with chorizo and ham back on the stove on medium heat and add the broth. Bring to a simmer and carefully break the eggs into the soup to poach for 2 minutes. Remove the eggs with a perforated spoon and set aside. Place a slice of bread into the bottom of each soup bowl and ladle the soup on top. Place a poached egg on top of each slice of bread and serve immediately. Yield: 4 servings. ❖

## Wine Suggestion

**Simi Rosé of Cabernet Sauvignon.** The red cabernet sauvignon grape is complex and quite versatile. In fact, it can produce a most flavorful and interesting dry rosé that is powerful enough to stand-up to fragrant or pungent herbs, vegetables, and smoked meats.

*The Spaniards love their rice and have their own version.
Produced in the marshlands around Valencia along the
Mediterranean coast, Spanish rice is of short-grain, similar to
Italian Arborrio rice.*

123

## Wine Suggestion

**Marqués de Riscal Rioja Reserva** is a fine accompaniment to veal, chicken, rich red meats (including game), and cheese. The Marqués de Riscal brought innovative French wine-making and viticultural techniques to Spain in the early 1800s.

# Grilled Veal Chops with Carrots, Brussels Sprouts and Tomato Bouquetières

*The Spanish enjoy their potatoes and Chef Noguera usually makes this dish with chunky french fries. We suggest boiling up quartered red or white potatoes and tossing them with butter and parsley. The tomatoes in this recipe are filled with peas — bouquetière-style.*

4   (8-ounce veal chops)
1/4  cup olive oil
     Salt and freshly ground pepper
4   small ripe tomatoes
6   tablespoons butter
1/2  cup fresh or frozen peas
1/2  cup baby carrots, cooked tender
1/2  cup Brussels sprouts, cooked tender
4   sprigs parsley for garnish

Brush one side of each veal chop with olive oil and place on a heated grill. Season the chops with salt and pepper. Cook for about ten minutes, or until the meat yields grill marks.

Meanwhile, prepare the tomato garnish or bouquetières. Bring a medium saucepan of water to boil and prepare an ice bath. Core the tomatoes and place in the boiling water for 35 seconds. Remove the tomatoes from the boiling water, plunge into a bowl of ice water and remove the skins and the top 1/3 of each tomato. Scoop out the seeds. Set aside.

In a small saucepan, heat 2 tablespoons of the butter until bubbly. Add the peas, coating them in the butter and heating through. Remove peas from the heat and spoon equally into the 4 tomato halves. Set aside and keep warm. Using the same saucepan, add the carrots and Brussels sprouts and heat through. Set aside and keep warm. Check the veal chops and turn over to cook on the other side. Remove each chop from the griddle and place on an individual serving plate with the tomato bouquetières, carrots and Brussels sprouts. Garnish with a few sprigs of parsley. Yield: 4 servings. ❖

# Cooking Beneath a Tapestry of History
## *Chef Juan Chavez*
### RESTAURANTE SALON REAL, SEVILLE

Chef Juan Chavez cannot remember a time when he was not busy in the kitchen, as early as teenage days and younger. Right after graduation from hotel school, he immediately was employed in running two restaurants. Interest-ingly enough, his concept of cooking has never wavered. "My philos-ophy has principally been based in using the natural ingredients of the earth," he describes.

His sherried tenderloin is a riot of fresh seasonings and of course, something from the garden – green beans. The sherry in the recipe takes advantage of the area's rich vineyards, and you will often find foods prepared flambé-style with a host of other yields from the ubiq-uitous rows of grapes the area produces. "Andalusian cuisine," he explains, "is based on the products we have in the gardens – vegeta-bles and greenery. We have plenty of fish from the lakes, and goat and pork from the moun-tains."

Spain is a melting pot of regions where the subtleties in cooking are there but may not be so obvious to the untrained palate. Chef Chavez explains, for example, how in his area, they roast their meats differ-ently from other Spanish provinces.

Hearty food, such as the gazpacho, is just what guests of Chef Chavez know they will enjoy as they come down from the windy ski slopes nearby and enter the restaurants at the Hotel Alfonso XIII.

Here, in one of the oldest and most ele-gant hotels in southern Spain, treasures from the past grace the decor: wood-carved ceilings, brightly colored tapestries, and colorful car-pets. The Moorish influence is ever-present, encouraging a palatial vacation spot all year long. The guest list is filled with celebrities from Princess Diana to the Gorbachev family, but everyone is welcome at this chef's very Andalusian table. ❖

*Spain has more vine-yard acreage than any other wine producing country in the world. Even though there are four million acres of vines planted, Spain actually produces less wine than either France or Italy.*

# Gazpacho Andaluz

*Served chilled, this traditional soup from Andalusia*
*offers a light, refreshing meal when the heat of summer becomes unbearable.*

## Wine Suggestion

**Simi Altaire.** A spicy and flavorful dish such as Gazpacho is complemented by the berry-like character of this medium-bodied red wine.

2  medium cucumbers, 1 peeled for the soup, the other diced into ¼-inch cubes and reserved for garnish

3  medium green peppers, seeded, 1 for the soup and the other diced into ¼-inch cubes and reserved for garnish

5  ripe, medium tomatoes, cored, 4 for the soup and the other one diced into ¼-inch cubes and reserved for garnish

3  cups hard-crust bread, diced into ½-inch cubes, with 1 cup reserved for garnish

2  cloves garlic, peeled
   Salt and freshly ground pepper

¼  cup extra virgin olive oil

3  tablespoons sherry vinegar

¼  cup red onion, peeled and diced, for garnish

¼  cup hard-cooked egg, diced for garnish

Prepare the soup by placing the cucumber, green peppers, and tomatoes into a blender or food processor. Process until smooth. Add the 2 cups of diced bread and the garlic cloves. Process again until well combined. Drizzle the oil and vinegar over all of the ingredients and season with salt and pepper. Blend until all of the ingredients are completely puréed and smooth. Pass the ingredients through a strainer or sieve, pushing down with a ladle to extract all of the juices.

Pour the soup into a tureen and refrigerate until ready to serve. When the soup is completely chilled, ladle it into a soup bowl and top with 1 teaspoon each of the garnishes. Yield: 6 servings. ❖

# Beef Tenderloin with Oyster Mushrooms and Green Beans in a Sherry Sauce

*Andalusia is renowned for its sherry, and chefs of the region have incorporated the wine into their recipes in unique and flavorful ways, such as the combination offered by Chef Juan Chavez.*

2  cups whole green beans, trimmed

1  pound beef filet, center cut from the tenderloin

Salt and freshly ground pepper

3  tablespoons olive oil

2  tablespoons butter

¼  pound oyster or button mushrooms

½  cup sherry

¾  cup beef stock

Cook the green beans in lightly salted boiling water for 4 to 5 minutes, until tender. Slice the filet into 4 equal portions and season with salt and pepper. Heat a skillet on high and add 2 tablespoons of the olive oil. Sauté the steaks for 2 minutes on each side.

Remove the steaks and set aside. Prepare the sauce. Add the butter to the pan and sauté the mushrooms with the remaining olive oil, until tender and still juicy. Pour off any excess fat and add the sherry. Reduce by half and add the stock. Reduce by half again. Place some of the green beans on each plate. Sprinkle with the mushrooms and add the steak. Spoon the sauce over the steak and serve.

Yield: 4 servings. ❖

## Wine Suggestion

**Marqués de Riscal Rioja Reserva.** Ruby-red in color with a distinctive black-cherry aroma and character, this Rioja Reserva, made primarily from the classic Tempranillo grape, makes a fine accompaniment to this well-seasoned dish.

# An Ancient Olive Oil Mill and 17th-Century Church Surround His Country Kitchen

## *Chef Erico Delgado*

### HOTEL HACIENDA BENAZUZA, SEVILLE

At one time, Chef Erico Delgado almost donned the white uniform of another profession. Although he was always in the kitchen – having been raised in a family where gastronomy was an art form – it was the field of dentistry that he found attractive enough to want to dedicate his life. But a year and a half into medical school, he discovered that something was missing. He longed for the kitchen, and the culinary life, so he pursued studies in France.

Today at the Hacienda Benazuza, guests are treated to the tastes of the Andalusia region, as Chef Delgado believes in creating dishes based on local products. Regional cooking – the chef believes – is what makes the difference and is, he adds, "the most important thing in the kitchen."

He also espouses the philosophy that great cooking is cooking that is done, "in the way you (the chef or cook) would like to eat it."

Chef Delgado also believes that ambiance is an integral part of the dining experience.

"We want our guests to take with them the memory that Benazuza is somewhat like their own home with a very attentive kitchen," adds the chef.

The Hacienda Benazuza, luxuriating in the sunny weather of this region, is enveloped by a gracious arboretum with exotic gardens and aromatic herbs. Gentle splashes from murmuring fountains complete the picture. History invites more of the magic with a 17th-century church and an old olive-oil mill, which are also part of the hacienda.

Located in a rural area a short distance outside of Seville, the hacienda is small – forty-four antiques-filled guest rooms – and dates to the 10th century when it was a Moorish estate.

In the Seville countryside, where red-tile roofs pop up above stucco walls the color of sand dust, and the crumbling tiled mosques and palaces bow to an opulent past, the enriched are those who get to sit at Chef Delgado's table or try his dishes at home. ❖

# Cold Tomato Soup with Glazed Scallions

*Spaniards are fond of starting a meal with soups, especially cold vegetable soups.*
*This soup is a delightful combination of ripe tomatoes and glazed, crunchy scallions.*

8 large ripe tomatoes, cored

3 tablespoons extra virgin olive oil

16 basil leaves, washed and patted dry

16 scallions, white part only, sliced thinly

Place a large saucepan filled with water on the stove on high heat and bring to a boil. Place the tomatoes into the boiling water for 35 seconds and remove to a bowl filled with ice water. (This prevents the tomatoes from cooking and makes removing the skins easier.) Once the tomatoes have cooled, remove the skins with a sharp paring knife. Slice the tomatoes in half, squeeze out the seeds and cut the tomatoes into wedges. Set aside.

Place a medium skillet on the stove over medium heat. Add 2 tablespoons of the olive oil and the tomato wedges, and sauté until soft to the touch. Remove the tomatoes from the skillet and place them in a blender or food processor. With the machine running, add the basil and purée until the tomatoes are a smooth liquid. Remove the soup from the machine and set aside in a bowl. In a medium skillet over medium heat, add the remaining olive oil and sauté the scallions until they begin to turn golden but still retain some of their crunch, about 5 minutes. Remove the skillet from the heat and set aside.

Pour some of the tomato soup into 4 soup bowls, dividing the soup equally. Top with some of the glazed scallions and serve. Yield: 4 servings. ❖

## Wine Suggestion

**Marqués de Riscal Sauvignon Blanc.** The excellent structure and flavorful nature of the Sauvignon Blanc grape will help to offset the piquancy that is contributed by the garlic and the spicy sausage in this delightful dish.

# Pineapple Tarts with Candied Citrus and Coconut Cream

*Refreshed with a candied citrus peel, this dessert is typical of the rustic, fruit and cream desserts popular in restaurants throughout Spain. The almonds add a nutty flavor, and note that some are sliced and the others finely ground.*

**Coconut cream:**

1¼ cups heavy cream

1 tablespoon sugar

½ cup freshly grated coconut

**Candied orange peels:**

1 medium orange, rind only, sliced into julienne strips

½ cup water

2 tablespoons sugar

3 tablespoons sliced almonds, toasted

**Batter:**

4 egg yolks

1 cup sugar

4 tablespoons butter, softened

1 cup finely ground almonds

**Pineapple preparation and assembly:**

1 tablespoon butter

1 medium pineapple, the tough outer skin, core and stem removed

1 tablespoon sugar

4 teaspoons cinnamon

Place a medium saucepan on the stove over medium heat and add the heavy cream, 1 tablespoon of the sugar, and the coconut. Bring the mixture to a boil, lower the heat to a simmer, and reduce by half, stirring constantly. When the coconut cream is reduced, remove the saucepan from the stove. Set aside and keep the coconut cream warm.

In a small, stainless steel saucepan, place the orange rinds, the water and 2 tablespoons of the sugar. Bring to a boil. Cook the syrup for 5 minutes. Add 3 tablespoons of the almonds and continue cooking for 5 more minutes over medium heat. Most of the liquid will be reduced when the peels are candied and ready for garnish.

While the orange peel is cooking, add the egg yolks and 1 cup of the sugar to the bowl of an electric mixer. Beat on high for 3 minutes. The yolks will turn pale yellow when they are ready. Stop the machine and gradually add 4 tablespoons of the butter, followed by the finely ground almonds. Mix until all of the ingredients are well combined. Set the mixing bowl aside.

Line a cookie sheet with aluminum foil and then brush the tablespoon of butter onto the surface. Set aside. Preheat the oven to 350°.

To prepare the pineapple, slice horizontal, ⅛-inch thick pieces, removing the fibrous center from each slice. Set the sliced pineapple aside and begin baking the tart.

Spread 2 tablespoons of the batter onto the cookie sheet, spreading each mound of batter out to the shape of a 2-inch circle. Be sure to keep at least 1 inch between each tart ring, for they spread. Place 1 ring of pineapple onto the surface of each circle, making sure to gently press the pineapple in the center to even the shape. Lightly sprinkle each tart with the remaining tablespoon of the sugar and all of the cinnamon. Bake in the oven for 10 minutes, or until the tarts are golden brown. Remove the tarts from the oven. Let settle for 2 minutes before removing from the cookie sheet. To serve, place 1 tart in the center of a serving plate, and garnish with the coconut cream, almonds and candied orange peel. Yield: 4 servings.  ❖

AUSTRIA

❖Salzburg

Vienna ❖

# AUSTRIA

# Cookery Books and Jazz Guitars:
# A Day in the Life of an Entrepreneurial Chef
## *Chef Ewald Plachutta*
### DREI HUSAREN, VIENNA

Not too far — about 50 kilometers — from his kitchen door, the sparkling waters of a famous river that inspired a classic waltz tune, *The Blue Danube,* embroider one of Austria's well-known vineyards. An endearing acquaintance of the chef works here in the Waucha vineyard village, an 80-year-old connoisseur known as the "grand tycoon" of wine-making in Austria.

In other corners of the world, he has more friends — some at the Mandarin and Oriental restaurants in Hong Kong; the Hotel Ritz in Barcelona; and the Hotel Gellert in Budapest, all premiere places where Chef Plachutta has worked.

Meanwhile, new friends are made all the time at Drei Husaren, where this worldly ambassador of good eating is not only the chef de cuisine, but a restaurateur. He owns part of Drei Husaren and two others, Hietzinger Brau and Grotta Azzura. Running businesses, plus finding time to strum on his guitar, and somewhere in between write a basic tutorial cookbook for aspiring home cooks, is just part of the multi-faceted life this great chef leads.

Central, however, to all of his ambitions and entrepreneurial pursuits, is creating fine cuisine. It tends to be very Austrian, a style that has been heavily influenced by the cookery of neighboring countries, especially Czechoslovakia and Hungary. The affection for pike, for example, can be traced to Poland. But the interpretation in the recipe here, including the strüdel, gives the dish its uniquely local character.

The popularity of the area's heavenly coffees can be credited to the Turks, who besieged Vienna more than once over the course of history. Taste a warm cup of local java with Chef Plachutta's towering Strawberry Napoleon, and you can imagine you are surrounded by old Vienna, re-created in the decor found at Drei Husaren. Taste one bite of his culinary works and Chef Plachutta can no doubt add another name to his long list of friends in every port. ❖

# Seafood Strüdel

*In Austria the term strüdel refers to both a dish and a type of dough. Savory fillings are as popular in strüdel as the traditional apple or sweet fillings. Here, you are making a stuffing of vegetables and then folding in a fish mousse. Chef Plachutta uses pike for this dish, as it is very available locally. But, you may use any white fleshy fish such as cod, perch, or whiting.*

## Stuffing:

3 tablespoons vegetable oil

³/₄ cup onions, minced

2 cups button mushrooms, minced

2 tablespoons chives, finely chopped

Salt and freshly ground pepper

## Salmon:

1 pound fresh salmon

## Seafood mousse:

8 ounces fresh cod, pike, or other white fish, cut into 1-inch cubes

1 egg, separated, white part only

¹/₃ cup heavy cream

## Assembly:

1 cup or more all-purpose flour

1 pound prepared puff pastry (or see page 164 to make it fresh)

## Egg wash:

1 yolk

2 tablespoons heavy cream

In a large skillet over medium flame, heat the oil. Add the onions, sautéing until they are translucent, about 5 minutes. Continue to stir the onions during cooking to prevent sticking and burning. Add the mushrooms and sauté for 30 minutes or until all of the excess moisture is removed from the mushrooms. Be careful not to let the mushroom mixture burn or stick. Add the chives and season with salt and pepper. Remove the skillet from the heat.

Prepare the salmon by slicing it lengthwise into 1-inch wide strips. Set the salmon aside and prepare the fish mousse. Place the cod into the bowl of a food processor or blender and add the egg white. Season with salt and pepper and with the machine running, slowly add the cream until a smooth, creamy sauce develops. Set aside and assemble the strudel.

Preheat the oven to 400°. Place 1 sheet of 9x13-inch puff pastry onto a floured work surface and roll to a thickness of ¹/₁₆ inch, making sure that the rolled sheet is an evenly shaped rectangle. Place the mushroom mixture on the bottom ¹/₄ of the sheet closest to the edge of the table. Using a pastry bag fitted with a plain tip, pipe the cod mousse on top of the mushroom mixture. Lay the salmon strips on top of the cod mousse and then cover the salmon with another layer of the cod mousse. Begin rolling the

*(continued)*

135

strüdel away from the edge of the work surface, making sure to fold in the edges along the side.

Place the strüdel on a cookie sheet lined with parchment paper or aluminum foil making sure the seam is tucked underneath the strüdel. This will prevent the filling from escaping during baking.

In a small bowl combine the yolk with the 2 tablespoons of heavy cream and brush the top of the strüdel. Bake in the oven 25 minutes or until the strüdel is golden brown. Remove the strüdel from the oven and slice into 2-inch thick slices, placing 2 slices each on individual serving plates. Serve immediately. Yield: 6 servings.  ❖

# Strawberry Napoleon

*Napoleon-style pastry is a classic Austrian sweet and so, in America, it has long been a favorite. This version with strawberries adds a new meaning to Napoleon.*

**Pastry:**

1 cup all-purpose flour

1 pound prepared puff
pastry dough or see page
164 to make it fresh

**Egg wash:**

2 eggs, lightly beaten

3 tablespoons heavy cream

**Strawberry cream:**

1/2 cup confectioners' sugar

2 tablespoons Grand
Marnier

1 1/2 cups heavy cream

1/2 cup strawberry purée
(blend of 1/2 pint fresh
strawberries)

**Assembly:**

1 cup whole strawberries

1 sprig mint for garnish

Confectioners' sugar for
garnish

Preheat the oven to 425°. Dust a work surface with some of the flour. Place 1 of the puff pastry sheets on top of the flour and roll out the sheet to 1/16 inch thick, making sure that an evenly shaped rectangle is formed. Set this aside and roll out a second sheet just like the first. With a 2-inch round cookie cutter, cut 12 (2-inch) circles from the puff pastry sheets. Any scraps can be wrapped in plastic and placed in the freezer to use in another recipe.

In a small bowl combine the eggs and heavy cream to form an egg wash. Set aside.

Place the 12 circles onto parchment or aluminum-lined cookie sheet, 1 inch apart. Brush the egg wash across the tops of each circle and place into the oven. Bake the circles until they are golden brown, about 5 to 10 minutes. Remove the circles from the oven and set aside to cool.

While the circles are cooling, begin preparing the strawberry cream. In a bowl of electric mixer with the whip attachment, whip together the confectioners' sugar, Grand Marnier, and the heavy cream. With the machine still running add the strawberry purée and slowly whip to loose peaks. As the cream begins to form peaks, raise the speed of the mixer to medium-high and whip until a stiff cream is formed.

Slice the 1 cup of whole strawberries individually into thin slices and set aside. Place the strawberry cream into a pastry bag fitted with a star tube and pipe

*(continued)*

# Wine Suggestion

**Sichel Trocken-beerenauslese.** Imagine completely shriveled grapes that look more like raisins, still growing on the vine in November or even December. They are overripe because they have been struck by "Noble Rot" (Edel-faule) and they are bursting with sweet concentrated grape juice. When made into wine, this juice explodes with flavors of ripe pear, peaches, apricots, and honey, unfurling a thick, almost maple syrup-like texture that coats the palate with a flood of sensations.

137

a small dime-sized mound onto the center of each serving plate. Place 1 of the rings onto each dot of cream and press to flatten. This will help keep the napoleon from sliding on the plate. Pipe a thin ring of mousse onto the pastry circle $\frac{1}{2}$ inch from the outer edge. Place some of the sliced strawberries on top of the mousse and cover with the second pastry circle. Press down very gently on the circle to hold it in place and level the layer of mousse underneath. Pipe another ring of mousse and strawberries just like the first layer and top with the final pastry circle. Pipe a large rosette of the cream in the center of the top pastry

layer and dust with confectioner's sugar. Garnish with a whole fanned strawberry and mint. Serve immediately. If you need to refrigerate this recipe, do not do so for more than 1 hour. Yield: 4 servings. ❖

# Looking a Fish in the Eye before You Buy . . .
## *Chef Stefan Hierzer*
### MAJESTAT AT THE HOTEL IMPERIAL, VIENNA

The culinary bouquet of Austrian specialties can be found in Chef Stefan Hierzer's dining room. During the day, locals and tourists alike stop at Austria's street corner sausage stands and pick up a quick snack or a strüdel. But when it comes to sitting down  to an elegant table for the evening, they flock to the Majestat at the Hotel Imperial for something individually prepared with a heavy emphasis on the natural.

"I don't like the natural flavor of food to be interrupted by something added," observes Chef Hierzer. Spices and herbs must be fresh. For example, he will even pass up fresh basil if it is in oil. Everything he adds to his dishes must be pure and unadulterated. Why, Chef Hierzer has even been known to reject fresh nutmeg if it is already grated as, "It has probably been finely grated and thus loses much of its flavor," he explains.

He is also particular about fish and recommends that you look at the eyes of the fish when shopping for seafood. They must be clear and the flesh pink in color so that you are assured of the quality. Finally, he suggests pressing your finger onto the fish. If the fingerprint impression remains, the meat is not fresh. It must bounce right back to receive Chef Hierzer's approval.

This kind of attention to detail is what has everyone returning to this Vienna landmark where the likes of Henry Kissinger, Queen Elizabeth, and Lee Iacocca have left their own impressions.

With recipes here such as the unusual potatoes with caviar and the scrumptious rendition of strüdel filled with grapes, you will have your own guests leaving their impressions on a very positive note also, naturally. ❖

# Boiled Beef Shoulder with Horseradish Cream

*Boiled beef is a traditional Austrian dish. It is usually paired with fresh horseradish in either a sauce or panade of bread, eggs, and cream as Chef Stefan Hierzer has done with this recipe.*

2    *pounds beef shoulder*

5    *peeled carrots: 3 halved lengthwise, 2 left whole*

1    *leek, halved lengthwise*

1    *medium celery root, cut into 1 ½-inch sections*

3    *whole bay leaves*

2    *tablespoons whole white peppercorns*

    *Salt and freshly ground pepper*

2    *cups (¼-inch cubes) stale bread*

1    *egg yolk*

4    *tablespoons heavy cream*

3    *tablespoons freshly grated, or (strained) prepared horseradish*

2    *tablespoons butter*

5    *tablespoons chopped fresh chives*

Fill a 4-quart stockpot half-full with water and heat to simmer. Add the shoulder, carrots, leek, celery root, bay leaves, peppercorns, salt and pepper. Cover and cook for 3 hours on medium heat at a slow simmer. There should not be any redness left to the meat. Set the meat aside, reserve the cooking broth, and keep warm.

Remove the leek, carrots, and turnip with a slotted spoon. Slice the 2 whole carrots into ⅛-inch slices, place into a medium saucepan and set aside. Slice 1 of the large segments of turnip into ⅛-inch slices and add to the saucepan with the carrots. Remove the shoulder and slice into 4 equal portions, ¾ inch thick. Set aside.

Pour 1 cup of the cooking broth from the shoulder into a medium saucepan and bring to a boil. Add the cubed bread and let stand for about 45 seconds to absorb the broth. Add ½ cup more of broth and salt and pepper, and whisk to form a heavy, wet paste. Add the yolk, heavy cream, and 2 tablespoons of the horseradish. Whisk to combine. Taste for flavor and season with salt and pepper if necessary.

Place the 4 slices of shoulder onto a cookie sheet and spread the bread mixture onto each slice, covering the entire surface of the meat. Place under a broiler and cook for about 4 minutes until the top of the bread mix has browned. Remove and set aside to keep warm.

While the bread is in the broiler, place the saucepan with carrots and celery root onto medium-high heat. Add the butter and sauté for about 2 minutes. Add 4 tablespoons of the beef broth, 2 tablespoons of the chives, and season with salt and pepper. Remove from the stove and spoon equal amounts of the vegetables onto the center of each serving plate. Place the slices of beef on top of the vegetables and sprinkle the remaining chives and horseradish for garnish. Serve immediately. Yield: 4 servings. ❖

*Red wine with fish, white wine with meat? Yes! Just keep in mind that wine and food pairings should reflect what you enjoy rather than some old established rule about what works. Many light-to-medium bodied red wines that have good levels of acidity are lovely when served with fish, especially those with firm flesh, like salmon, swordfish, tuna, and marlin. The corollary to this is that rich, full-bodied or particularly flavorful white wines can be delicious accompaniments to red meats.*

# Grape Strüdel

*Chef Hierzer has created a light, refreshing filling for traditional strüdel that is sure to please any dessert lover.*

## Wine Suggestion

**Sichel Eiswein.** The remarkable concentration of fruit in an Eiswein (Ice Wine) will enhance the grape flavor and balance nicely with the delicate pastry. Eiswein can be enjoyed with lighter desserts or on its own before or after a meal.

1   pound green seedless grapes

2   eggs, separated

1/2   cup sugar

2   tablespoons pure vanilla extract

1/4   teaspoon cinnamon

2   ounces chopped walnuts

1/4   cup all-purpose flour, plus 1/2 cup or more for dusting

1   pound prepared puff pastry or see recipe on page 164 to make it fresh

1   egg slightly beaten

Confectioner's sugar for garnish

1 1/4   cups sabayon sauce (see recipe on page 111), warmed

Fresh mint for garnish

To begin, slice all of the grapes in half, place in a bowl and set aside. Place the 2 whites and 2 yolks into separate mixing bowls of an electric mixer. Add 4 tablespoons of the sugar to the yolks and beat them on high speed until a froth begins to form. With the machine running, add the vanilla and cinnamon. Whip until light and airy. Set the bowl aside. With the machine on high speed, whip the whites to a soft foam and add the remaining sugar in 3 stages, whipping the whites to stiff, shiny peaks. Remove the bowl from the machine and set aside.

Place the walnuts and grapes into the bowl with the yolk mixture and mix well. Fold 1/3 of the whites into the yolk and walnut mix, combining gently without collapsing the whites. By adding part of the egg whites to the yolk mixture the yolks are not as heavy and won't collapse the other egg whites when they are added. Fold in the remaining egg whites and gently fold the flour in 3 batches, combining well between each addition. Set this bowl to the side and prepare the puff pastry.

Preheat oven to 425°. Dust the work surface with flour and roll out 1 of the 9x13 sheets of dough to an evenly shaped rectangle, 1/16 of an inch thick. Brush the puff pastry with some of the beaten egg and pour the strüdel filling along the bottom edge of the dough closest to the edge of the table. Fold the sides up on each end to encase the filling, and begin rolling the dough onto itself. The seam at the bottom edge should be on the underside. Place the strüdel on a cookie sheet lined with parchment paper or aluminum foil, making sure the seam is underneath the strudel to prevent the filling from escaping during baking. Brush the outside of the strüdel with more of the beaten egg. Bake the strüdel until it turns an even golden brown, about 30 minutes.

When ready, remove the strüdel from the oven and set aside to cool for 2 minutes. Dust the top of the strüdel with powdered sugar. Slice the strüdel into 1 inch thick slices, and place on a serving plate. Garnish with some of the sabayon sauce and fresh mint. Serve while still warm. Yield: 6 servings. ❖

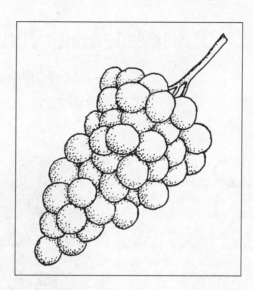

# Renegade Youth Turns Renaissance Chef
## *Chef Reinhard Gerer*
### KORSO RESTAURANT, VIENNA

*"Simplicity is not the same as being simple, and quality need have nothing to do with being complicated."*

*– Gerer*

Reinhard Gërer was born in 1953 in Zeltweg, an industrial town in the southern part of Austria. At fifteen, he began cooking in an amusement park where quantity, not quality, was everything.

In 1968, Reinhard began his culinary education in Vienna, but proved to be a non-dedicated student caught up in the youth revolution where books of progressive literature became more important than cookbooks. He finally committed to a career and gathered experience working in many world-class kitchens in Vienna. His first real chef's job was at Le Pialet where he received his first toque from Gault Millaut. A year later, he received another, plus one star from the Michelin Guide. He is now known for taking luxury restaurants and putting them on the map far beyond the Austrian borders.

Today, Chef Gerer has written two cookbooks, has been awarded three toques, and has been in charge of the Korso at the Hotel Bristol since the restaurant opened its doors at the 100-year-old hotel. In 1992, he was named Austrian chef of the year and at least one European magazine has rated his, one of the ten best restaurants in the world. It is not difficult to realize that Chef Gerer is an individual. It's clear from his handwritten menus to the design of the Korso as a replica of the elegant dining room on the Titanic. And his special cuisine has been tagged by gourmands as "the most creative of the creative."

Vienna houses one of the largest factories in the world. So the recipe here for Lemon Noodles with Caviar can certainly be considered not only an original Gerer, but a nice example of what you might find in his part of the world on a daily basis.

If you had to sum up what makes Chef Gerer so successful and sought out, you would have to point to something he said and perhaps learned many years ago at the amusement park: "Simplicity is not the same as being simple, and quality need have nothing to do with being complicated." ❖

# Pasta and Caviar in a Lemon and Cream Sauce

*The smooth richness of this sauce and the saltiness of the caviar make for an interesting blend of simple, yet complex flavors – and what an exciting easy way to serve pasta.*

## Wine Suggestion

**Sichel Piesporter Goldtröpfchen.** The variety of lush fruit and good acidity from the Riesling grape allows this wine to be served with such diverse ingredients as lemon and caviar. This wine is made from grapes that come from the Goldtröpfchen (little drops of gold) vineyard which is located in the village of Piesport.

1   pound fresh pasta such as linguini or angel hair

3   tablespoons butter

2   tablespoons grated lemon zest

2   tablespoons grated lime zest

½   cup sour cream

½   cup beef stock

4   tablespoons heavy cream
    Salt and freshly ground pepper

4   tablespoons Sevruga caviar, or salmon caviar

Place a large saucepan filled with salted water on the stove on high heat and bring to a boil. Cook the pasta al dente, or for about 5 minutes. Remove the pan from the stove and drain the pasta.

In a large skillet over medium heat, melt the butter and add the grated lemon and lime zest. Sauté the zest for 1 minute to infuse the butter with the flavor of the zest. Add the pasta. Stir the pasta well so that it is completely coated with the butter and zest. Remove the skillet from the stove and keep the pasta warm.

In a medium mixing bowl, combine the sour cream, stock, and heavy cream together with a whisk to form a smooth sauce. Spoon this mixture into the skillet with the pasta and put the skillet back on the stove on medium-low heat, cooking until all of the ingredients are heated completely through. Continue to stir all of the ingredients well to form a smooth coating. Season with salt and pepper.

Divide among 4 serving plates. Spoon 1 tablespoon of caviar on each plate of pasta and serve immediately. Yield: 4 servings. ❖

# Emperor's Pancakes with Lemon and Berry Sauce

*Although this is a dessert dish in Austria, you may wish to serve it for
an elegant breakfast or brunch, or afternoon tea.*

## Wine Suggestion

**Sichel Beerenauslese.** The ripe fruit richness of this dessert wine makes it eminently compatible with the berries, raisins, and cinnamon in the recipe. The richly layered flavors and thick texture are the result of a very selective picking of late-harvest grapes only.

### Batter:

- 1 cup sour cream
- ½ cup all-purpose flour
- 2 tablespoons confectioners' sugar
- 2 eggs, separated
- 1 tablespoon grated lemon zest
- ⅛ teaspoon salt
- 3 tablespoons golden raisins
- 2 tablespoons butter, melted

### Fruit sauce:

- 1 cup strawberries, core and leaves removed and cut in half
- 1 cup raspberries
- ¼ cup granulated sugar

### Garnish:

- Confectioners' sugar for garnish
- 4 tablespoons pistachios, coarsely chopped

In a medium bowl, mix together with a spatula, the sour cream, flour, sugar, yolks, zest and the salt. Set aside. In bowl of an electric mixer, whip the egg whites on high speed until soft peaks form. Gently fold ⅓ of the egg whites into the sour cream mixture and completely combine. Fold in the raisins and then the remaining egg whites, being careful not to deflate the whites. Set aside and cook the pancakes.

Preheat the oven to 150°. In an 8-inch nonstick skillet, melt the butter over medium heat. Pour enough batter into the sauté pan to form a 3-inch circle. When the bottom is golden brown turn the pancake over and cook on the other side. As each pancake finishes cooking, place it in the oven to keep warm until ready to serve.

While the pancakes are cooking, place the strawberries, raspberries, and ¼ cup sugar into a small saucepan to cook on low heat. Stir the sugar and berries to combine. Cook the berries until they are soft and a sauce forms, about 5 minutes. Remove the pancakes from the oven and place 3 on each serving plate. Drape each pancake with berry sauce. Garnish with a sprinkling of confectioners' sugar and the pistachios. Serve immediately. Yield: 4 servings. ❖

# Cool Lakes and Mountains of Music in the Land of the Waltz and Schnitzel

## *Chef Herbert Pöcklhofer*

### HOTEL GOLDENER HIRSCH, SALZBURG

Wolfgang Amadeus Mozart was born here, and directly across from the Hotel Goldener Hirsch is a cultural center that holds festivals in his honor. This is after all, Salzburg, a home of classical music. They flock to this luminary city for its symphonies, but also for compositions of the culinary kind performed by Chef Herbert Pöcklhofer.

While the strains of the great artists are heard in the festival hall, they sing the praises of one of Austria's finest chefs in a hotel whose origins date to 1407. Back then it was the *Güldener Hirsch* and it served as a meeting place for international society. Although its physical attributes have changed over the years, its philosophy has not. Guests are surrounded by unpretentious luxury where antiques create the individual decor. Even the bar was made from an antique trunk and there is a table from an ancient monastery refectory.

Rich and lively music has influenced the Austrian character and vice-versa. The charm and wit found in the country's legendary waltzes is expressed in its people as well as its cuisine from dumplings to schnitzels and sweet strüdels.

In Chef Pöcklhofer's kitch-en, main courses are dominated by game from local forests, thus the inspiration for the delicious Venison in a Brandied Fruit Sauce. As lakes, rivers, and mountains abound here, the food tends to come from crystal waters and rugged terrain, producing pike, perch, char, salmon, and trout and the lamb, beef, and splendid cheeses.

Chef Pöcklhofer serves up Austrian specialties at the hotel with award-winning aplomb. He has worked in many countries and was selected to represent Austria in the *Bocuse D'or* in Lyon. He was a finalist in the Prix Tattinger two years in a row.

Lengthening shadows cast their images on the music world at the cultural center. But across the way, the talents of a busy chef eclipse those images with a set of their own impressive silhouettes. ❖

# Venison in a Brandied Fruit Sauce

*A veritable cornucopia of fruits and spices teases the venison with great flavors. The juniper berry spice is a mainstay of Scandinavian cooking and is also used in the making of wines and spirits.*

## Wine Suggestion

**Simi Cabernet Sauvignon Reserve.** Game and cabernet sauvignon lead to a heavenly marriage, particularly when ginger and a cranberry sauce are included in the recipe. A combination of power and elegance are found in this Cabernet Reserve with well-developed flavors of blackberries, cassis, cedar and plums.

1   tablespoon black peppercorns
10  whole juniper berries
3   bay leaves
2   tablespoons fresh rosemary and more for garnish
3   tablespoons fresh thyme
1   teaspoon salt
4   tablespoons vegetable oil
1   pound venison scraps
1   carrot, peeled and coarsely chopped
1   medium celery root, peeled and coarsely chopped
1   tablespoon tomato paste
1   leek, green part only, coarsely chopped
1   cup red wine
6   cups water
1/3 loaf dark brown bread, cut into 1-inch pieces (about 1cup)
1   medium orange
2   teaspoons currant jelly
1   tablespoon Dijon-style mustard
2   teaspoons jellied cranberry sauce
2   tablespoons all-purpose flour
1   tablespoon brandy
1/4 cup Kirsch
1   cup heavy cream
1   pound venison, cut into 4 equal portions

Using a mortar and pestle, coarsely grind together the peppercorns, juniper berries, bay leaves, rosemary, thyme, and salt. Set aside. In a large saucepan over medium-high heat, heat the 2 tablespoons of the vegetable oil and venison scraps, cooking until well browned. Add the carrots and celery root, and sauté five minutes. Stir in the tomato paste and add the leek, cooking for 2 minutes to tenderize the ingredients and combine their flavors.

After 5 minutes deglaze the saucepan with the red wine and simmer for 5 more minutes to reduce and intensify the stock. Add the water, making sure to cover the meat and vegetables completely. Add the bread to the stock.

Cut the orange in half and squeeze the juice of 1 of the halves into the stock, followed by the orange rind, the currant jelly and the reserved dry spice mix. Stir the stock to combine all the ingredients well. Lower the heat and simmer for 2 hours.

After 2 hours, remove the stock from the stove. Pour into a strainer and into a medium saucepan. Simmer on low heat. Whisk the mustard and cranberry sauce into the reducing sauce. While the sauce is reducing further, place a medium bowl on the table and add the flour, brandy, 1 tablespoon oil, and the Kirsch. Whisk all of the ingredients until free of lumps. Slowly whisk this into the reducing sauce, whisking briskly to prevent lumping. Allow the sauce to cook for 5 minutes to cook out the flour taste. Remove the saucepan from the heat and pour through a strainer into a clean saucepan. Heat the sauce over a very low flame, adding the cream, and whisking well to prevent curdling. Let the sauce cook for about 5 more minutes. While the sauce is cooking, place a skillet on the stove on medium heat. Add the remaining oil. Rub both sides of the venison with salt and pepper and sauté each side for 3 minutes to brown. Remove the venison from the skillet and place into the simmering sauce. Let the venison stew in this sauce for 5 minutes to tenderize the meat and impart the flavors of the sauce. Remove the venison to individual serving plates. Drape with the sauce and garnish with the rosemary. Yield: 4 servings. ❖

*Celery root is the root of a vegetable called celeriac or celery rave. Peel celery root as you do most root vegetables.*

# Braised Red Cabbage

*Try this traditional Austrian dish as an alternative to boiled cabbage.*
*Its pungent flavors go well with both meat and poultry.*

1   medium head red cabbage,
    shredded

½   cup apple juice

½   cup fresh lemon juice

3   tablespoons apple cider
    vinegar

¼   cup red wine

1   teaspoon caraway seeds

2   tablespoons butter

2   tablespoons all-purpose
    flour

    Salt and freshly ground
    pepper

Marinate the cabbage in a medium bowl with the apple juice, lemon juice, apple cider vinegar, red wine, and the caraway seeds. Let marinate for a minimum of 10 minutes or ideally overnight. In a medium saucepan over medium flame, melt the butter. Add the flour and whisk to combine to form a roux. Cook the roux for 5 minutes, stirring constantly. Add the cabbage mixture to the cooking roux and mix well. Season with salt and pepper. Cook the cabbage until tender, about 5 minutes. Remove the cabbage from the saucepan and place into a serving bowl. Serve immediately. Yield: 4 servings. ❖

# An Old Farmhouse Inspired a Life of Cooking and Commitment
## *Chef Ingrid Häupl*
### HOTEL HÄUPL, SALZBURG

Ingrid Häupl has been cooking professionally for some 30 years, and all in the same place. A new graduate, training in the field of hotel management in Vienna, she took a vacation with her parents one year in the Salzburg countryside and virtually never left.

The Hotel Häupl was the lodging for the family sojourn. Originally, the hotel, with its Italian castle-like architecture and complementary Italian furniture, was a farmhouse, bakery, and inn up until World War II. It was here that Ingrid met Hans and they were married a year later. Now, she is in the kitchen and her husband helps run the small hotel, as did six generations of the Häupl family before him.

Chef Häupl trained with Ernst Faseth, who for ten years was president of the "World Association of Chefs." But she also credits her culinary knowledge and skill to her mother-in-law. Ingrid's style of cooking, which has earned the restaurant two toques, is light Austrian where frozen foods are prohibited and vans of fresh produce arrive daily for the picking of the chef. Meats also are brought to the door — from individual butchers for lamb, beef, and poultry.

The chef enjoys treating her dinner guests to dumplings, which reign supreme in Austria but can be found in what has been referred to as "the dumpling belt," stretching from Alsace to Poland. Dumplings may be served as savories or sweets as they are prepared in many ways: as a part of stews; as the main course; as dessert; or added to soups such as the one here by Chef Häupl.

When she is not busying her trained hands in the kitchen, the chef finds enjoyment in playing bridge or serving away from the restaurant — on the tennis court.

The Häupl tradition is a steadfast one. The eighth generation has embarked upon the inspirations of the old farmhouse. Ingrid and Hans' daughter, Veronika, who has spent five years in a hotel-training school, is already involved in helping to run the hotel. She's proving that a new career and commitment are on the horizon for Hotel Häupl. ❖

# Wine Suggestion

**Ruffino Santedame Chianti Classico.** A medium bodied, dry red wine can work quite nicely with a richer soup. Soft fruit and velvety texture make this wine suitable for other dishes, such as rich red meats, chicken, veal, and fish.

# Oxtail Soup with Semolina Dumplings

*If oxtail (used because of great flavor) is hard to find, substitute with beef bone. You will be clarifying the soup by employing a technique called clarification raft. The process removes grains, fats, and other excess food particles that cause the cloudiness. They will float to the top of the broth, hence the suggestion of a raft.*

**Broth:**

| | |
|---|---|
| 1 | tablespoon vegetable oil |
| 10 | pounds oxtails, cut into equal portions |
| 1 1/2 | cups leeks, coarsely chopped plus 1/2 cup for the raft (see below) |
| 1 1/2 | cups carrots, peeled and coarsely chopped |
| 1/4 | cup parsnip, peeled and coarsely chopped |
| 1 1/2 | cups celery root |
| 2 | tablespoons whole black peppercorns |
| 2 | tablespoons whole juniper berries |
| 3 | bay leaves |
| 12 | cups water |

**Clarification raft:**

| | |
|---|---|
| 6 | egg whites |
| 2 | pounds lean ground beef |
| 1/2 | cup carrots, finely chopped |
| 1/2 | cup leeks, finely chopped |
| | Salt and freshly ground pepper |

**Dumplings:**

| | |
|---|---|
| 2 | tablespoons soft butter |
| 1 | reserved egg yolk, slightly beaten |
| 2 | cups semolina flour |
| 1/2 | cup sour cream |
| 1 | bunch chives for garnish |

Add the vegetable oil to a 1-gallon stockpot and heat on high. Add the oxtails and sauté until browned, about 5 minutes. Add the 1 1/2 cups leeks, carrots, parsnips, celery root, peppercorns, juniper berries, bay leaves, and water. Simmer on low heat for 25 minutes. Remove the stock from the stove. Strain through a sieve and pour into a clean stockpot, keeping warm on medium heat.

Separate the eggs, placing the whites into a large mixing bowl. Reserve 1 yolk for the dumplings and the other yolks for another recipe. Whisk the whites until they are frothy. Add the ground beef, carrots, and leeks, and season with salt and pepper. Mix these ingredients thoroughly and then fold into the hot stock, stirring gently. (It is important not to break up the clarification raft or let the stock come to a hard boil. This can cause the soup to become cloudy.) The clarification process should take about 20 minutes.

While the soup is clarifying, prepare the dumplings. Begin by whisking the softened butter in a mixing bowl to form a smooth paste. Gradually incorporate the egg, continually whisking to keep the mixture smooth. Scrape the sides of the bowl to incorporate any lumps and break them up. Add the semolina flour and sour cream, and whisk briskly to combine. Season with salt and pepper and chill for 1 hour.

When the clarification raft is ready to be removed, it will be firm and floating on top of the soup. The bubbles will be clear. Remove the raft with a slotted spoon and strain the soup through the strainer lined with cheese-cloth or coffee filter into a clean saucepan. Keep warm on low heat until ready to serve. (This will catch any loose particles or fat that were missed in the clarification.)

Place a small saucepan on the stove on high heat and fill with water. Remove the dumplings by moving the mixture back and forth between 2 spoons. Poach the dumplings in the water on the stove for 7 minutes.

Remove with a slotted spoon and place into individual soup bowls. Ladle the soup onto the top of the dumplings and garnish with fresh chives. Yield: 6 servings. ❖

# Spiced Bread Soufflé

*This is a traditional Austrian dessert, often called Tipsy Monk when it has a liquor, such as rum added. Chef Häupl has simplified the recipe for those who prefer to cook without alcohol.*

3   eggs, separated

⅔   cup granulated sugar

¼   teaspoon ground cloves

½   teaspoon cinnamon

1   teaspoon grated lemon zest

½   cup walnuts, finely chopped

¾   cup plus 2 tablespoons fine bread crumbs

1   tablespoon butter, softened

1   cup prepared sabayon sauce or see recipe on page 111 to make it fresh

Confectioners' sugar for garnish

Fresh mint for garnish

In a bowl of electric mixer, beat the egg whites on high, slowly adding ⅓ cup of the sugar in 3 stages. Beat the whites until stiff, shiny peaks form. In a separate bowl, beat the yolks on high, adding the remaining sugar in 3 stages. Beat the yolks until pale yellow and firm. To the yolks, add the cloves, cinnamon, zest, walnuts and the ¾ cup of bread crumbs. Gently fold this mixture into the egg whites, being careful not to collapse the whites. Set aside and prepare the baking dish.

Preheat the oven to 350°. Brush the inside of a 9x5-inch casserole dish with the softened butter. Pour in the remaining bread crumbs. Lift the casserole to distribute the bread crumbs over the entire surface of the casserole. Spoon the batter into the casserole and spread the top evenly with a rubber spatula.

Set the casserole into a roasting pan filled 1-inch deep with hot water. Bake 20 minutes or until the top becomes a pale golden brown. Remove the roasting pan from the oven and set the casserole onto the table. Allow to cool for 5 minutes, and then run a sharp knife along the outer edge of the casserole. Slice horizontally into 2-inch strips. Turn the casserole around and cut 2-inch strips vertically. Place 2 of the rectangles onto each serving plate, and serve with sabayon sauce. Garnish with the powdered sugar and mint. Serve immediately. Yield: 4 servings. ❖

# PANTRY
## RECIPES

# Tomato Concassée

*This basic recipe for chopping tomato pulp can be used in
a number of Italian and Provençal sauces.*

2   medium tomatoes (about
    1 pound)

Bring a medium saucepan of water to a boil. Stem the tomatoes and score the bottom with an X. Parboil the tomatoes in the water for 20 to 30 seconds or just until the scored edges of the skin begin to peel back. Transfer the tomatoes to a cold water bath to stop the cooking. Once they are cool enough to handle, cut the tomatoes in half horizontally, squeeze out the seeds, peel off the skin and chop into a small dice. Yield: 1 ½ cups. ❖

*Place the flat side of the tomato (or any more elliptically shaped fruit or vegetable) down on the cutting board to make it easier to cut. Cut tomatoes vertically first, then across.*

# Basil Mayonnaise

2   egg yolks
2   tablespoons dijon mustard
    Salt and freshly ground pepper
⅓   cup olive oil
1   large basil sprig
10  basil leaves, cut into thin
    strips

Separate the eggs and add the yolks to a small bowl. Add the mustard and salt and pepper to taste, and whisk well to combine. Add the olive oil in a thin stream, whisking to combine the oil and the egg yolks to form an emulsion. (An emulsion is when the oil combines with the egg yolks and binds with it to form a thick sauce.) The oil must be added slowly or it will not be absorbed by the egg yolks. Add basil leaves to the mayonnaise. Yield: 1 cup. ❖

# Caesar Salad with Croustades

**Croustades:**

1   head romaine lettuce,
    washed and patted dry,
    cut into bite-size pieces

2   cups (2-inch dice) white
    French bread

¼   cup olive oil

3   cloves garlic, minced

¼   teaspoon dried basil

    Salt and freshly ground
    pepper

**Anchovy paste dressing:**

12  oil-packed anchovy filets,
    drained, rinsed, and
    patted dry and thinly
    sliced

1   clove garlic, minced

2   hard-cooked egg yolks
    (reserve whites for
    another recipe)

2   tablespoons fresh lemon
    juice

½   cup olive oil

    Salt and freshly ground
    pepper

½ - ¾  cup freshly grated
    Parmesan cheese

Wrap the romaine lettuce in a damp towel and refrigerate until ready to toss with the dressing. Sauté the diced bread in the olive oil with the garlic cloves. Shake the pan well and cook over medium heat until the croustades are delicately browned. Toss with the basil and cook until crisp. Season with salt and pepper. Remove the garlic and drain the croustades on paper towel.

Make the anchovy paste dressing. In a chilled salad bowl, mash the anchovies and garlic together to make a paste. Beat in the yolks and lemon juice until smooth, beating constantly with a wire whip, slowly adding the olive oil. Season to taste with salt and pepper.

Place the romaine leaves into the bowl and toss gently, making sure to combine all of the ingredients. Add the croustades and Parmesan and toss again. Serve immediately. Yield: 6 servings. ❖

**The Hennessy
Martini.** This classic
can be enjoyed as an
apéritif.

*Recipe:*
- Fill a shaker with ice
- Add 2 oz. of
  Hennessy V.S and
  squeeze in 1 lemon
  wedge ($^1/_2$ tsp.)
- Stir gently, don't
  shake
- Let settle
- Strain into a chilled
  martini glass
- Garnish with a
  lemon peel

# Sautéed Pimientos with Ham

*The uses for this recipe from Chef Noguera are many, from serving with bread or cheese
as an appetizer to a side dish for beef or poultry.*

4   tablespoons olive oil

4   medium cloves garlic,
     coarsely chopped

$^1/_2$   pound Serrano ham or
     Prosciutto, diced into $^1/_4$
     inch cubes

8   red bell peppers, roasted,
     peeled, seeded, and sliced
     julienne

     Salt and freshly ground
     pepper

Heat the oil in a deep skillet over medium-high
heat. Sauté the garlic until just golden. Add the ham
and sauté just until it begins to turn golden. Add the
peppers to the pan, swirling to combine the ingredients. Season with salt and pepper. Pour the peppers
onto a plate and serve. Yield: 4 servings.  ❖

# Sautéed Cabbage with Bacon

*This is a great, simple recipe for cabbage from Chef Erico Delgado.*
*This can be served as a side dish to many main courses.*
*It is easy to do and adds a pleasing, crunchy texture and smoky flavor.*

12  large cabbage leaves
12  thin slices bacon
    Salt and freshly ground
    pepper to taste

Bring a 2-quart saucepan of water to a boil over high heat. Add the cabbage leaves and cook for 5 minutes, until the leaves are tender. Remove the cabbage from the water and plunge into ice water to stop the cooking process. Pat the cabbage dry with a paper towel and cut it into bite-size pieces.

Chop the bacon into $1/4$-inch pieces and place in a skillet on medium-high heat. Sauté the bacon until the meat becomes golden brown. Add the chopped cabbage. Stir to combine and continue to sauté until the bacon has become dark brown and crisp, and the cabbage is translucent. Season with salt and pepper and remove the cabbage from the skillet. Place into a large serving bowl and serve immediately.

Yield: 4 servings. ❖

**Hennessy V.S.O.P
Privilège Cognac.**
Take the chill off a
crisp fall or winter
evening by serving a
glass of V.S.O.P (Very
Superior Old Pale).

# Baked Potato Caviar

*Chef Huysenstrugt plays a clever trick on our palates by pairing the smooth texture of the potato
with the grainy saltiness of the caviar. This elegant dish is quick and easy to make.*

6   medium baking potatoes,
    scrubbed with the skins
    intact

6   tablespoons butter

    Salt and freshly ground
    pepper

6   tablespoons caviar

6   small clusters of fresh mint

6   teaspoons chopped chives

Preheat the oven to 350°. Bake the potatoes in
the oven for 40 minutes or until they are very soft on
the inside. Remove the potatoes from the oven and
place them on a cutting board. Cut each potato in half
horizontally, slicing a small wedge from the bottom of
each half so that it rests squarely on the plate. Scrape
the flesh out of the potatoes and place the pulp into a
small saucepan with the butter. Season with salt and
pepper and stir well to combine into a smooth paste.
Spread the puréed pulp onto each of the potato
halves. Place on a serving plate, top each potato with
1 teaspoon of caviar and garnish with mint and
chopped chives. Serve while the potatoes are still
warm. Yield: 6 servings. ❖

# Brown Sauce or Sauce Espagñole

*Recipes often call for a brown sauce, especially red meats and game. You may make this ahead of time as it freezes well. Brown sauce is called a mother sauce because as a base or foundation, many other sauces can be made by the addition of a few new ingredients.*

**Mirepoix:**

3  onions, diced

4  carrots, diced

4  ribs celery, diced

**Roux:**

¹/₂  cup butter

¹/₂  cup all-purpose flour

**Sauce base:**

3  quarts homemade beef stock

¹/₂  cup tomato purée

**Bouquet garni:**

1  bay leaf

1  sprig thyme

4  parsley stems

Place a large stockpot on the stove with the onions, carrots, and celery. Add the butter and heat on medium-high. Sauté the vegetables until well browned but not burned. Add the flour and stir to make a roux or paste. Cook the roux until it is browned and the flour cooks away.

Whisk in the stock and the tomato purée and bring to a boil, stirring constantly. Reduce the heat to simmer and skim the surface of any foam or small particles. (Never let the stock come to a rolling boil or the sauce will become cloudy.) Tie together the ingredients for the bouquet garni, using kitchen string. Add the herb bundle to the stock and let simmer for about 2 hours or until the sauce is reduced to about 6 cups. Skim the surface often.

Once reduced, remove the pot from the stove and pour into a strainer lined with several layers of cheesecloth. Press gently on the mirepoix to remove the juices. Chill quickly in a bowl nested inside another bowl of ice water to prevent the spread of bacteria and eliminate the growth of a skin on the surface. Yield: 3 quarts. ❖

*When a recipe calls for a non-reactive sauce-pan or baking dish, it is necessary because acidic ingredients present in the recipe combine with metals, such as aluminum, and can affect the color and flavor of the dish.*

*The mirepoix, the roux, and the bouquet garni are the elements of the recipe. Mirepoix is a mixture of rough cut vegetables, herbs and spices used to flavor stocks, soups and sauces. A roux is a combination of flour and butter used to thicken many types of sauces. Bouquet garni is usually a combination of herbs tied together to prevent from disbursing in a liquid. The "bouquet" is removed before serving.*

161

# White Butter Sauce or Beurre Blanc

*White butter sauce is a nice accompaniment to grilled,
baked or steamed fish or shellfish.*

1   shallot, minced

⅓   cup white wine vinegar
or white wine

1   stick butter, sliced

    Salt and freshly ground
pepper

In a small, nonreactive saucepan, boil the shallot and vinegar over high heat until the liquid is reduced to about 1 tablespoon.

Lower the heat to medium. Whisk in the butter, piece by piece, adding fresh butter just as the butter in the pan melts. Season to taste with salt and pepper and cook until the sauce is emulsified, thick and creamy.

Remove the pan from the heat and use the sauce immediately, or cover it and keep it warm for no longer than 2 hours over a double boiler. Yield: ⅔ cup sauce. ❖

# Fish Stock

2 - 3   pounds fish bones or
frames

2 - 3   quarts water

      Salt

(If using whole fish frames, gut them, remove the gills and wash them as well as the fish bones under cold running water. Cut them to fit in the stockpot.)

Put the fish bones in a large, nonreactive stockpot. Add water to cover, about 2 to 3 quarts, and salt to taste. Bring to a boil and skim the scum as it rises. Reduce the heat, cover the pot, and simmer for about 20 minutes.

Strain the stock through a colander, removing the bones. Cool, cover and refrigerate or freeze until ready to use. Yield: 1½ quarts. ❖

# Chicken Stock

2  pounds raw or cooked
   chicken meat and/or bones

2  quarts water

2  stalks celery, cut into 1-inch
   pieces

1  carrot, cut into 1-inch pieces

1  onion, cut in half

1  bay leaf

2 - 3  parsley stems

6  peppercorns

   Salt

Put the chicken in the stock pot. Add the water, celery, carrot, onion, bay leaf, parsley, peppercorns, and salt to taste. (When salting the chicken stock, some of the liquid will evaporate and the stock will become more concentrated. Be careful not to oversalt). Bring to a boil and skim the scum as it rises. Reduce the heat and partially cover and simmer the stock for 1½ to 2 hours. Add more water if the liquid evaporates and the bones or vegetables are not covered.

Strain the stock through a colander into a large bowl and cool it uncovered. Refrigerate the stock and remove the congealed fat from the surface. Store the stock in the refrigerator for several days or freeze it in smaller containers. Yield: 1½ quarts. ❖

# Basic Vinaigrette

1  tablespoon vinegar

   Salt and freshly ground
   pepper

3  tablespoons olive oil

Pour the vinegar into a small bowl. Season to taste with salt and pepper. Whisk in the oil. Yield: ¼ cup. ❖

# Quick Puff Pastry

*Unlike traditional puff pastry, this recipe is less labor intensive. It may be used for both savory and sweet pastry cases. The secret to good puff pastry is not to let the butter get too cold or hot because uneven distribution can cause excessive fat run-off during baking. Be sure to read the directions thoroughly before beginning.*

**Hennessy Paradis Cognac.** A sublime spirit that descends softly and finishes with flavors that appear to be finely woven like an intricate lace pattern. Paradis (Paradise) is aged slowly in oak barrels and contains blends of Cognac, some of which are more than 100 years old.

12 ounces unsalted butter (very cold)

1 1/2 cups all-purpose flour

1/2 cup cake flour

1 teaspoon salt

1/2 cup ice water

Preheat the oven to 400°. Dice the butter into 1-inch squares and place into an electric mixing bowl with the flours and salt. (Make sure that the butter did not get warm while dicing, if so refrigerate until cold.) Mix the dough on low speed with the paddle attachment, until the butter is broken into 1/2-inch pieces (the size of chickpeas). Mix in just enough of the water to hold the dough together without making the butter pieces any smaller.

Lightly flour a flat work surface. Quickly roll the dough out to a 12-inch rectangle, making sure the dough is still cold. At this point the dough will not have come together yet and will look unevenly mixed. Fold 1/3 of the rectangle over the center, and fold the remaining 1/3 on top of the first fold. Lightly flour the top of the dough and turn it 90 degrees so that the length becomes the width. (The dough must be turned like this before each roll so that the gluten is pulled evenly to prevent deformities when baked.) Lift up the dough and lightly sprinkle flour underneath, taking up any dough that may be stuck to the work surface.

Flour the top of the dough and roll it into a rectangle a second time, making sure the surface of the dough is smooth and even. Do not handle the dough excessively or press down on the dough when rolling out; the heat from your hands can melt the butter. Remove any excess flour

from the surface of the dough and fold the 2 ends to the center. Make sure the corners are even and have square edges.

Fold the dough in half like a closed book to complete the procedure. Refrigerate about 15 minutes to chill the butter and relax the gluten. Repeat the folding process twice more, remembering to chill the dough if necessary. When ready to use, remove from the refrigerator and roll out to a 12-inch rectangle $1/16$-inch thick. Cut into desired shapes. Yield: 3 pounds. ❖

# Crème Anglaise

*This vanilla custard sauce is useful for many recipes.*

12  egg yolks

1  cup sugar

4  cups milk

1  tablespoon pure vanilla
   extract

In a bowl of electric mixer, combine the yolks and sugar. Beat with the whip attachment until thick and light. In a heavy saucepan, bring the milk and vanilla to boil. With the mixer running on low speed, very slowly pour the milk into the yolk mixture and combine.

Return the milk-and-egg mixture to the saucepan and turn down the heat to medium-low. Heat the mixture slowly, stirring constantly to prevent burning and lumping. Prepare a bowl filled with ice water. When the sauce begins to thicken and coats the back of a wooden spoon, remove the saucepan immediately from the heat and scrape custard into a stainless steel bowl. Place custard-filled bowl into the bowl filled with ice water. Stir the sauce frequently to speed the cooling process. By placing the sauce over ice, the cooling process is sped up and bacteria less likely to grow. Once the sauce is completely cooled, refrigerate until ready to use. Yield: $2^{1}/_2$ pints. ❖

*To cut an apple or any round fruit or vegetable, slice in half, turning cut sides down. Slice each piece and then cut across to dice.*

# Sugar Syrup

*Use the sugar syrup to poach fresh or dried fruits or berries.*

2   cups granulated sugar

½ -1   cup water

In a medium saucepan, bring the water to a boil, stirring to dissolve the sugar. Determine the amount of sugar to use based on the sweetness of the fruits or berries you are using.

Flavor the syrup to match its use. Possible flavorings are: vanilla, wines, liqueurs and other spirits, citrus fruits and peel, and herbs and spices. Yield: 2 cups syrup. ❖

*Prehistoric man made sweet foods of syrup from maple and birch trees, honey, fruits, and seeds. Over the centuries, it was finally the Crusaders who really advanced the opportunity for sweets as we know them today. Crusaders discovered sugar cane and developed puff pastry.*

# Pastry Cream

*This is a basic recipe for filling pastries and an assortment of other desserts.*

4 eggs

2 egg yolks

1 ¼ cups sugar

½ cup cornstarch

1 quart milk

1 tablespoon pure vanilla
    extract

½ cup sugar

2 ounces unsalted butter

In a medium mixing bowl whisk together the eggs, egg yolks, and ½ cup of the sugar, mixing well. Add the cornstarch and whisk to remove any lumps. Set aside.

In a heavy stainless steel saucepan, dissolve the remaining ¾ cup sugar in the milk and vanilla, and bring just to a boil. Slowly pour half of the milk-and-vanilla mixture into the egg mixture, while whisking. (This brings the temperature of the egg mixture equal with the milk and prevents curdling.) Pour this mixture back into the saucepan with the other half of the milk and reduce the heat on the stove to low. Bring to a slow boil, stirring constantly to prevent burning and lumping. (At this stage the pastry cream will start to thicken rapidly and it is important that it be briskly stirred at all times.)

The pastry cream should be thick and stick to the back of a spoon when done. Remove immediately from the stove and place into the bowl of a mixer with the paddle attachment.

Add the butter and beat on medium speed until completely cooled. (This prevents the growth of bacteria and cools the cream quickly to stop the cooking process.) Once cooled, place into a shallow container and cover with plastic wrap, directly touching the surface of the pastry cream. This prevents a tough outer skin from developing. Refrigerate for at least 2 hours before use.
Yield: 1 quart. ❖

**Hennessy X.O Cognac.** This is comprised of a blend of Cognacs, some of which are 70 years old.

# Chocolate Ganache

*Ganache is a rich chocolate filling or coating that may be used to fill pastries and meringues, or glaze and fill cakes. Use high quality chocolate to ensure that the taste is smooth and melts easily on the tongue.*

2  *cups heavy cream*

8  *ounces semisweet or bitter sweet chocolate, finely chopped*

Place the chopped chocolate into a medium stainless steel bowl and set aside. In a heavy medium saucepan, heat the cream over medium-high heat until it simmers. Pour the cream into the chocolate and stir until partially melted.

Let sit for approximately 15 minutes to allow all of the chocolate pieces to melt completely. Stir the mixture again until smooth and there are no lumps. Be careful not to stir the ganache too much as it is melting or it will become grainy and separate. At this stage the ganache can be used as a sauce, write a greeting atop a cake, or use as a glaze.

To chill ganache, cover with plastic wrap to prevent a skin from forming and refrigerate until very cold, 8 hours or overnight. Once cold, it can be whipped in a mixer and used to fill cakes, or scooped directly from the refrigerator to make chocolate truffles. Yield: 2 ½ cups. ❖

# Fruit Purée

*Use as a sauce with pastry, ice cream and fruit desserts.*

1 pint strawberries ($^3/_4$ -1 pound), washed and hulled

2 tablespoons sugar

Whirl together the strawberries in a food processor or blender until puréed. Strain for a smoother purée. Yield: 1 cup. ❖

# Raspberry Sauce

*As a general rule, most fruit sauces such as raspberry, begin with a purée.*
*This sauce is very easy to make and can be used with ice cream as well as baked desserts.*

3 cups ripe raspberries

$^1/_2$ cup sugar

2 tablespoons fresh-squeezed lemon juice

2 tablespoons raspberry liqueur (optional)

Pour the raspberries into a food processor or blender and chop coarsely. With the machine running add the sugar, juice, and liqueur and purée until smooth. Strain the purée through a sieve to remove all of the seeds. Taste for sweetness and if necessary add more sugar. Yield: approximately $2^1/_2$ cups. ❖

# Braised and Caramelized Endive

*When you caramelize sugar, be sure to use a heavy pan. If using a copper pot, you must use a special sugar-cooking pan. The sugar gets so hot that it can actually melt.*

4   *Belgian endives*
    *Salt and freshly ground pepper*
1   *lemon*
2   *tablespoons water*
2   *tablespoons butter*
1   *teaspoon olive oil*
2   *teaspoons sugar*

Preheat oven to 325°. Place endive into a saucepan and season to taste. with salt and pepper. Squeeze the juice of half a lemon into the pan using a sieve to catch the seeds. Add 2 tablespoons water and 1 tablespoon butter to the pan. Create a loose fitting cover out of aluminum foil and cover the endive. Braise for 30 minutes.

When the endive is cooked, drain on a cooling rack. Add one teaspoon olive oil to a nonstick skillet and place on high heat. Slice the endive in half lengthwise. Add one tablespoon butter and one teaspoon sugar to the skillet. Add the endive, sliced side down, and one teaspoon additional sugar. Turn to brown evenly and carmelize, about three minutes per side. To serve, cut off the base of the endive and fan each out on a dinner plate. Yield: 4 endives.  ❖

# RESTAURANT
## D I R E C T O R Y

*Jean Bardet*
**Jean Bardet**
57 Rue Groison
37100 Tours, France
Phone: 33 47 41 41 11

*Christophe Blot*
**Le Royal Champagne**
Bellevue
51160 Champillon, France
Phone: 33 26 52 87 11

*Juan Chavez*
**Restaurante Salon Real**
Hotel Alfonso XIII
San Fernando, 2
41004 Seville, Spain
Phone: 34 5 422 2850

*Gulio Corti*
**Dolci and Dolcezze**
P.zza Beccaria, 8/R
50121 Florence, Italy
Phone: 39 55 23 45 458

*Bernard Dance*
**Château de Saran**
Chouilly
51200 Epernay, France
Phone: 33 26 57 53 76

*Erico Delgado*
**Hotel Hacienda Benazuza**
Virgen de las Nieves S/N
41800 Sanlucar la Mayor
Seville, Spain
Phone: 34 5 570 3344

*Alfredo Del Peshio*
**Harry's Bar**
Calle Vallaresso
1323 Venice, Italy
Phone: 39 41 52 85 777

*Alain Ducasse*
**Louis XV Restaurant**
Hotel de Paris
Place du Casino
Monte Carlo, Monaco 98000
33 92 16 69 21

*Annie Féolde*
**Ristorante Enoteca Pinchiorri**
Via Ghibellina 87
Florence, Italy
Phone: 39 55 24 27 77

*Alain Finkbeiner*
**La Grangelière**
59 Rue Du Rempart Sud
68420 Éguisheim, France

Phone: 33 89 23 00 30
*Reinhard Gerer*
**Korso Bei Der Oper**
Mahlerstrasse 2
A-1010 Vienna, Austria
Phone: 43 1 51 516 546

*Celestino Giacomello*
**Hotel Gritti Palace**
Campo S. Maria Del Giglio, 2467
Venice, Italy
Phone: 39 41 79 46 11

*Jean-Claude Guillon*
**Bel-Air Cap-Ferrat**
6230 Saint-Jean-Cap-Ferrat
Côte d'Azur, France
Phone: 33 93 76 50 50

*Ingrid Häupl*
**Häupl**
A-4863 Seewalchen Am Attersee
Haupstrasse 20-22
Salzburg, Austria
Phone: 43 7662 22 49

*Stefan Hierzer*
**Hotel Imperial**
Kärntner Ring 16
A-1015 Vienna, Austria
Phone: 43 1 50 110 0

*Luc Huysentruyt*
**De Snippe Restaurant**
Nieuwe Gentweg 53
Brugge 8000, Belgium
Phone: 32 50 33 70 70

*Didier Lefeuvre*
**Château d'Isenbourg**
68250 Rouffach, France
Phone: 33 89 49 63 53

*Guy Legay*
**Hotel Ritz**
15, Place Vendome
75001 Paris, France
Phone: 33 1 42 60 38 30

*Dominique Le Stanc*
**Chanteler Restaurant at Hotel Negresco**
37 Promenade Des Anglais
B.P. 379 06007 Nice,
France Cedex 1
Phone: 33 93 88 39 51

*Jean-Michel Lorain*
**La Côte Saint-Jacques**
14 Faubourg de Paris
B.P. 197
89304 Joigny, France
Phone: 33 86 62 09 70

*Valentino Marcattilii*
**Ristorante San Domenico**
Via Gaspare Sacchi, 1
40026 Imola, Italy
Phone: 39 542 290 00

*Bernardo Santos Garcia-Muñoz*
**Café de Oriente**
Plaza de Oriente, 2
Madrid, Spain
Phone: 34 1 541 3974

*Antonio Gistau Noguera*
**Hotel Santa Maria De El Paular**
28741 Rascafria
Madrid, Spain
Phone: 34 1 869 1011

*Serge Philippin*
**Restaurant Le Bacon**
Boulevard Bacon
06600 Antibes, France
Phone: 33 93 61 50 02

*Ewald Plachutta*
**Drei Husaren**
Weihburggasse 4
A-1010 Vienna, Austria
Phone: 43 1 512 10 92

*Herbert Pöcklhofer*
**Hotel Goldener Hirsch**
Getreidegasse 37
A-5020 Salzburg, Austria
Phone: 43 662 84 85 11

*Arnaud Poëtte*
**Eden Roc at Hotel Du Cap**
Boulevard Kennedy
06602 Antibes, France
Phone: 33 93 61 39 01

*Hervé Raphanel*
**La Maison d'Maitre**
Hotel Conrad Brussels
Avenue Louise 51
1050 Brussels, Belgium
Phone: 32 2 542 42 42

*Francisco Rubio Sanchez*
**Palace Hotel Madrid**
Grill Neptuno Restaurant
Plaza de las Cortes, 7
28014, Madrid, Spain
Phone: 34 1 429 7551

*Giovanna Folonari-Ruffino*
**Ruffino's Tuscan Experience**
Chianti Ruffino
Esportazione Vinicola Toscana Spa
Via Aretina, 42/44 - 50065 Pontassieve
Tuscany, Italy
Phone: 39 55 83 68 307

*Emile Tabourdiau*
**Hotel Le Bristol**
112 Rue Du Faubourg St. Honoré
75008 Paris, France
Phone: 33 1 42 66 91 45

*Jean-Louis Taillebaud*
**Ecole De Gastronomie Francaise**
Hotel Ritz
15, Place Vendome
75001 Paris, France
Phone: 33 1 42 60 38 30

*Joseph Thuet*
**Le Trianon**
9 Avenue de Champagne
51200 Epernay, France
Phone: 33 26 54 71 21

*Pierre Wynants*
**Comme Chez Soi**
Place Rouppe Plein, 23
Brussels 1000, Belgium
Phone: 32 2 512 29 21

# INDEX